totally cool
Polymer Clay Projects

totally cool

Polymer Clay Projects

Marie Browning

Sterling Publishing Co., Inc.
New York

PROLIFIC IMPRESSIONS PRODUCTION STAFF:

Editor in Chief: Mickey Baskett
Copy Editor: Phyllis Mueller
Graphics: Dianne Miller, Karen Turpin
Styling: Sarah Patrey
Photography: Jerry Mucklow, John Yanyshyn
Administration: Jim Baskett

Library of Congress Cataloging-in-Publication Data

Browning, Marie.
  Totally cool polymer clay projects / Marie Browning.
     p. cm.
  Includes index.
  ISBN 1-4027-0642-1
  1. Polymer clay craft. I. Title
TT297 .B77 2004
731.4'2--dc22

                                                            2003023993

10 9 8 7 6 5 4 3 2

Published by Sterling Publishing Co., Inc.
387 Park Avenue South, New York, N.Y. 10016

© 2004 by Prolific Impressions, Inc.

Produced by Prolific Impressions, Inc.
160 South Candler St., Decatur, GA 30030

Distributed in Canada by Sterling Publishing
c/o Canadian Manda Group, 165 Dufferin Street
Toronto, Ontario, Canada M6K 3H6
Distributed in Great Britain and Europe by Chris Lloyd at Orca Book
Services, Stanley House, Fleets Lane, Poole BH15 3AJ, England
Distributed in Australia by Capricorn Link (Australia) Pty. Ltd.
P.O. Box 704, Windsor, NSW 2756 Australia

Printed in China
All rights reserved
Sterling ISBN 1-4027-0642-1

About Marie Browning

Marie Browning has made a career of designing products, writing books and articles, and teaching and demonstrating. Many products that you see in your favorite craft store, such as stencils, stamps, transfers, soap-making kits, and a variety of other products for arts and crafts may have been designed by Marie Browning.

She is the author of five books on soapmaking: *Totally Cool Soap Making* (Sterling 2004), *300 Soap Recipes* (Sterling 2002), *Beautiful Handmade Natural Soaps* (Sterling, 1998) and *Melt & Pour Soapmaking* (Sterling, 2000). In addition to books about soapmaking, Browning has authored other books published by Sterling: *Handcrafted Journals, Albums, Scrapbooks & More, Hand Decorating Paper, Jazzy Jars, New Paper Crafts, Wonderful Wraps, Making Glorious Gifts from Your Garden,* and *Memory Gifts*. Her articles and designs have appeared in *Handcraft Illustrated, Better Homes & Gardens, Canadian Stamper, Great American Crafts, All American Crafts,* and in numerous project books published by Plaid Enterprises, Inc.

Marie Browning earned a Fine Arts Diploma from Camosun College and attended the University of Victoria. She is a Certified Professional Demonstrator, a professional affiliate of the Canadian Craft and Hobby Association, and a member of the Society of Craft Designers, and Hobby Industry Association.

She lives, gardens, and crafts on Vancouver Island in Canada. She and her husband Scott have three children: Katelyn, Lena, and Jonathan. Marie can be contacted at www.mariebrowning.com. ❏

ACKNOWLEDGMENTS

Many thanks to everyone who helped and supported me for this book – photographer John Yanyshyn and my assistant Gloria Davenport; my editor, Mickey Baskett; and my family, husband Scott and children Katelyn, Lena, and Jonathan.

Thanks also to the following companies for generous contributions of product and support:

- For Fimo brand polymer clay, polymer clay tools: *American Art Clay Co. Inc. (AMACO), 4717 W. 16th St., Indianapolis, IN, www.amaco.com*

- For colored wire: *Artistic Wire, 1210 Harrison Ave., LaGrange Park, IL, ww.artisticwire.com*

- For decorative edge children's scissors: *Fiskars, 7811 W. Stewart Ave., Wausau, WI, www.fiskars.com*

- For Sculpey and Premo brands polymer clay, eraser clay, flex clay, polymer clay tools: *Polyform Products, 1901 Estes Ave., Elk Grove Village, IL, www.sculpey.com*

- For magnets: *The Magnet Source, 607 Gilbert, Castle Rock, CO, www.magnetsource.com*

- For Kato brand polymer clay: *Van Aken International, Rancho Cucamonga, CA, www.katopolyclay.com*

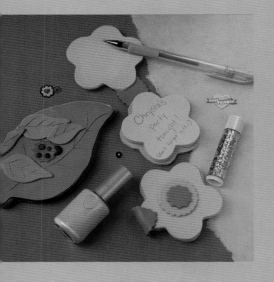

Contents

The technique of molding and firing clay to form vessels and other artifacts is almost as old as civilization itself. Prehistoric men and women dug up moist, pliable clay from the earth and discovered that if the clay were formed into vessels, left to dry, then baked in a fire, the vessel could hold water.

Although some of the tools have changed and we now work with a new type of clay, the essence of working with clay is not very different – we still use our hands and imagination to form beautiful and useful objects. In this book, you'll learn how to create with this new clay, using many of the same techniques that have been passed down for thousands of years.

The new clay is called polymer clay. It was developed in Germany in the late 1930s and was used to create doll heads and miniatures for doll houses. Later it was sold in toy stores as a toy for children but was not widely available in North America until the 1970s, when American companies started manufacturing it. (Colors weren't added until the early 1980s!)

Today polymer clay is available in a wide selection of beautiful colors and effects. Best of all, it can be baked in a home oven – a kiln is not required. New specialty polymer clays such as eraser clay and flexible clay expand the creative possibilities.

The book is filled with fun and practical projects that make wonderful gifts. An adult can help you bake your clay creations in your home oven after you have finished modeling them. Have fun!

Marie Browning

SAFETY FIRST

Like just about everything in life, the important first step is to read all the instructions, and the second important step is to follow them. This is especially true when it comes to safety. Raw, unbaked clay and baked polymer clay is completely safe to handle, but do not put it in your mouth! Use common sense and follow these important safety rules:

- **Never** put raw or baked clay in your mouth.
- **Don't** make items that will hold food or beverages.
- Wash your hands with soap and water before and after handing the clay.
- Always open a window while baking clay.
- Use an oven thermometer (found at hardware and kitchen stores) to make sure you are baking the clay at the exact temperature recommended by the manufacturer.
- Burning clay will create toxic fumes. You can bake the clay pieces longer, but never in a hotter oven than specified by the clay manufacturer.
- **Never** use a microwave oven to bake the projects.
- Anything you use from the kitchen for polymer clay must **not** be used for food preparation. These items include the cutting knife, cookie cutters, and rollers. There are toxins from the stabilizers in the clay that remain on all utensils that you use, no matter how well you wash them. Mark these tools "Polymer Clay Use Only."
- Keep children under 8 years of age and pets away from the polymer clay.
- Birds are very sensitive to the fumes that are released while the clay is baking. Be sure to take them out of the room.
- **Only adults** should use the sharp cutting tools. With adult supervision, children can use paring knives.
- **Never** apply pressure to the top edge of a polymer clay blade.
- When sanding polymer clay, wear a dust mask and "wet sand" the clay to minimize dust.
- **Always** clean your hands thoroughly after working with polymer clay.

About Polymer Clay

What is Polymer Clay?

Polymer clay is moldable plastic that you bake in your home oven to cure and harden. It is not earth clay (like ceramic clay) but is, instead, a man-made material. Here are some points and tips about creating with polymer clay:

- *It's safe.* Polymer clay is safe to use if you follow the instructions.
- *There's a huge variety.* Polymer clay comes in lots of colors, and you can mix colors together to make more. There are also translucent clay, fluorescent-colored clay, stone-effects clay, and colored glow-in-the-dark clay.
- *Look at specialty clays, too.* Some polymer clays are soft, some are stiff. Most of the brands sold in children's kits are nice and soft and easy to condition. Specialty clays especially good for children include eraser clay (which can be used as an eraser after baking) and flexible clay (very strong polymer clay that bends like rubber without breaking after baking).
- *You can mix them.* All polymer clays are made of similar formulas and can be mixed together. Mix them well so they do not separate.
- *You can use the leftovers.* No clay is ever wasted. As you make projects, you will start to have a pile of odd pieces in strange, multicolored hues. This clay can be used to make tools or as bases for larger items.
- *You can re-bake it.* You can embellish baked pieces with fresh, unbaked clay and re-bake over and over.

Working with Clay

- If tools are sticking to the clay, brush a little cornstarch on the clay.
- If the polymer clay is sticking to your hands, wipe your hands with baby oil.
- Polymer clay can be molded, sliced, rolled into balls, or flattened into sheets. It can be stamped and textured and holds fine details well.
- After baking, polymer clay can be drilled, painted, sanded, or glued.

Storing Polymer Clay

Polymer clay contains no water to allow it to dry out so the clay remains soft until you bake it. Proper storage will keep your polymer clay fresh and easy to work with.

To store, wrap polymer clay in wax paper and place in sealable plastic bags. Don't let the clay touch plastic bags or containers – polymer clay can dissolve plastic. The clay should be stored in a cool place, unexposed to direct sunlight. Refrigeration or freezing can extend its shelf life considerably. If you live in a warm climate and your house is not air-conditioned, the clay may become partially cured in the summer months. Properly stored, the clay can last for years.

Polymer Clay Tools

You don't need lots of special tools to work with polymer clay — the very best tools are your own hands. The items shown, many of which can be found in your home, are useful:

1. **Modeling tools** - Available where polymer clay is sold. They are inexpensive and very handy for detailing and smoothing out the clay.

2. **Wooden skewers** - Different lengths and thicknesses are available in grocery stores. Use them to hold beads while baking and to aid in rolling different thicknesses of clay sheets.

3. **Wooden toothpicks** - Use round ones to make holes in beads and add fine details.

4. **Cutting tools** - Thin **polymer clay knives** are great for making thin slices. *Caution:* Only adults should use these thin, sharp blades. Never apply pressure to the top edge of the blade, and grasp the sides when using.

   Craft knives are handy for cutting out shapes from clay sheets. Again, *only adults* should use these sharp knives.

   Inexpensive **paring knives** – ones without serrated edges – are my favorite cutting tool when working with children. The ones you can buy in "dollar stores" are very cheap and not at all sharp; they provide a good cut and are easy for children to handle. Adults you know best – if children can handle a knife at the dinner table, they can probably handle a paring knife when working with polymer clay.

5. **Rollers** - Clear acrylic rollers can be found at craft stores with polymer clay. They provide a smooth surface that clay does not stick to when rolling out the thin clay sheets. *Options:* Inexpensive plastic rollers; a strong glass bottle or a plastic core from a fax paper roll. Wooden rolling pins are not suitable – they are not smooth enough and the clay sticks to the wood.

   A **pasta machine** that can be dedicated to polymer clay only is great fun to use and makes rolling sheets and conditioning the clay really fast. However, a pasta machine is rather expensive if you are only doing a few projects.

6. **Cornstarch** and a **soft brush** - Brush cornstarch on polymer clay before impressing with a rubber stamp or texture tool – it keeps the clay from sticking.

7. **Measuring tools** - An ordinary ruler is used to cut straight sides and to measure polymer clay coils into evenly divided pieces for making perfectly matched beads. The six-sided polymer clay ruler is a fast and easy way to make perfect marks on clay coils. Simply press lightly into the clay and cut along the marks.

8. **Aluminum foil** is used to prop up pieces while baking and to form the insides of large clay pieces. A foil core makes pieces lighter and uses less clay.

9. **Hand-wipes** for cleaning hands, tools, and work surfaces.

10. **Polymer clay varnish** and **craft brushes** give baked pieces a gloss or satin finish. I recommend using a waterbased varnish made by the polymer clay manufacturer when working with children.

11. **White craft glue** and **glue brushes** for gluing raw clay on surfaces such as glass, paper mache, card paper, and plastics.

12. **Index cards or card paper** can be used to bake finished items on and to make templates.

Work Surface

Ceramic Tiles: I like to use inexpensive ceramic tiles as smooth working surfaces. Children can work on them and bake the items on them. An 8" x 10" glazed tile is a good size. Cover your work area with **newspaper or freezer paper** to protect it from the clay.

Tools for Decorating Clay

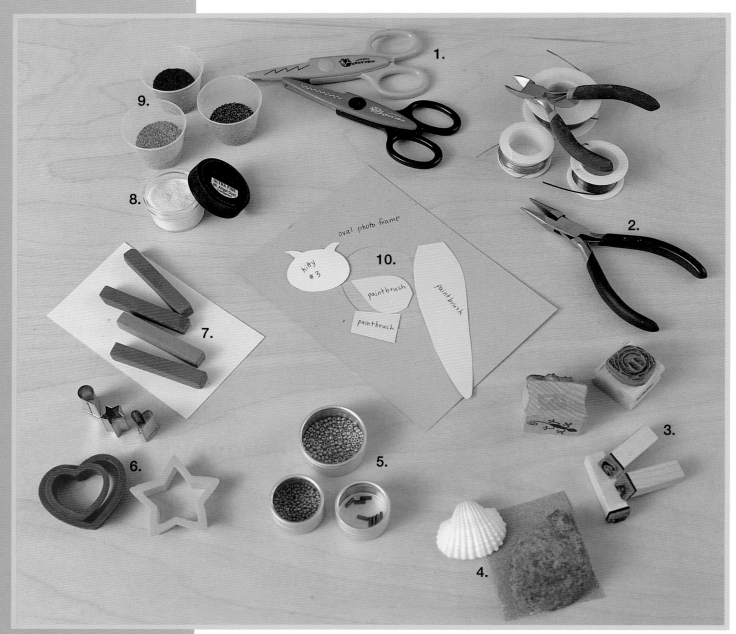

oval photo frame

kitty #3

10.

paintbrush

paintbrush

paintbrush

1.

2.

3.

4.

5.

6.

7.

8.

9.

These decorative tools are great to have –

1. **Decorative edge scissors** can be used to cut the clay into fancy pieces. Brush the clay lightly with cornstarch to prevent sticking. Clean the scissors by wiping with a paper towel.

2. **Colored wire** and tools for working with wire – **pliers** and **wire cutters**. Use wire to add curly antennae on a bug or to make a loop for a pendant.

3. **Rubber stamps** are great for impressing designs in clay. Alphabet sets are especially handy when working with children.

4. **Found objects** such as **shells, rocks, or sandpaper** can be used to add texture to clay.

5. **Beads** can be pressed in soft, unbaked clay for added interest. Use only glass (not plastic) beads with raw clay.

6. **Cookie cutters** are great for cutting neat shapes quickly. Inexpensive plastic cutters come in nesting shapes and are especially easy for children to work with. Brush the clay with a light coating of cornstarch to prevent sticking. Clean the cutters by wiping with a hand wipe – you can even find small cutters with plungers for pushing out the cut clay piece. Remember: Tools used for polymer clay cannot be used with food. Very small cutters come in handy for smaller, more detailed work. TIP: If you cannot find cookie cutters in the shapes you like, cut the shapes from index cards and use as templates for cutting shapes.

7. **Chalk pastels** can be brushed on the clay with a clean brush for beautiful shaded color effects. Inexpensive tempera paints or powder makeup also can be used.

8. **Glitter** adds sparkle to clay. It can be brushed on raw clay before baking or sprinkled on wet varnish after baking. For best results, use very fine glitter with raw clay – it won't work if the glitter is too coarse. TIP: Always test your glitter on a piece of clay to make sure it can withstand oven temperatures.

9. **Spices like seasoning salt, chili powder, and poppy seeds** can be mixed into transparent clay for wonderful stone effects.

10. **Card templates** are easy to cut out using the patterns at the end of this book.

they add that special touch to clay projects.

Handmade Tools for Decorating

Making your own sculpting tools is a great idea – it uses up leftover clay and is an inexpensive way to create useful tools.

Texture Tools

Look in your button box for buttons with interesting textures and novelty shapes to use as texture tools.

Here's How:

1. Roll a small piece of leftover clay into a short, fat coil.
2. Push the button (metal or plastic) or a metal stud on one end. *Note:* I have tried many different plastic buttons and all have baked fine with no melting.
3. Form the handle of the tool by squeezing with your thumb and forefinger.
4. Bake the clay to harden.

Stamping Tools

Pencil erasers and pieces of wire can be used to stamp designs in clay. Adults can use a sharp craft knife to carve the tops of new pencil erasers into simple designs. Use thick (18-gauge) wire coiled into a design to make the wire stamps.

Smile Tool

Younger children especially enjoy the smile tool – it quickly presses perfect "smiles" in clay. Make several for a wide variety of sizes and shapes – they can also make eyebrows and faces with a variety of different expressions.

Here's How:
1. Roll a small ball of leftover clay.
2. Flatten one side of the ball really thin and curve into a U shape.
3. Bake the clay to harden. (You won't know how it looks until you bake it – some will work out better than others.

Heart Tool

This tool is great for making perfect hearts! Make it about 3" long so it will make a variety of heart sizes.

Here's How:
1. Roll leftover clay into a fat coil.
2. Press the coil flat on the surface while pinching the top.
3. Bake to harden.

To make a heart:
1. Roll a small amount of clay into a ball.
2. Form the ball into a teardrop shape and flatten slightly.
3. Press the wide end of the shape into the point of the heart tool.
4. Form the bottom into a point. Add a wire loop to make a heart pendant.

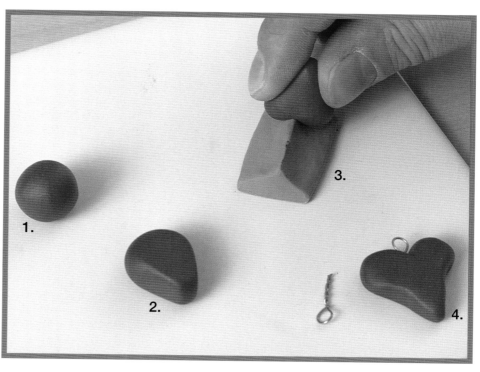

Creative Supplies

Here are some of the creative supplies that were used to embellish the projects in this book. Look for them at craft stores, at stationery shops, and around your home.

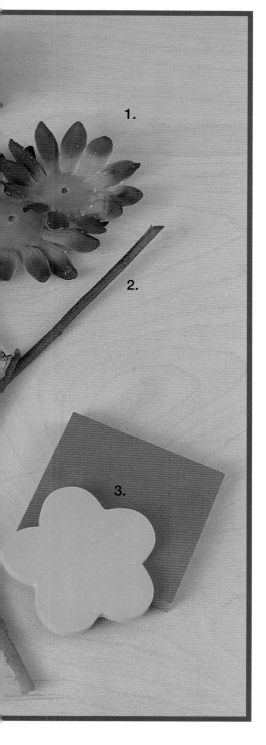

1. **Silk flowers**

2. **Twigs** (You can gather them in your yard or from houseplants.)

3. **Sticky note pads** - They come in lots of colors and shapes.

4. **Jewelry findings** like split rings, brooch backs, lanyards, small rings, lobster clasps, crimp beads.

5. **Magnet strips** for making decorative magnets.

6. **Pencils** - They are fun to decorate and give as gifts

7. **Pens** - There are so many fun pens available to decorate.

8. **Beads** - Use glass beads and plastic beads along with the polymer clay beads you make.

9. **Papier mache boxes** - These are inexpensive and great for decorating with clay.

10. **Feathers** - These will add a whimsical touch to your creations.

11. **Glass bottles and glass vases**, recycled from your kitchen.

12. **Wooden clothespins**, the spring type.

13. **Cording**, for stringing beads.

14. **Push pins**, in assorted colors.

15. **Paper clips**, both large and small.

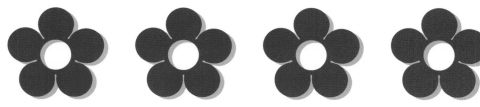

About Color

The Color Wheel

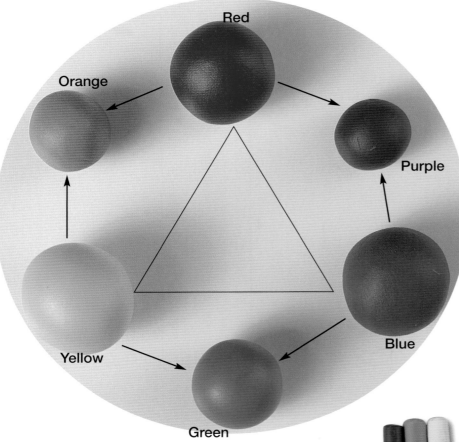

The color wheel shows the three primary colors: red, yellow, and blue. These colors cannot be mixed from other colors, but you can mix the primary colors to make the secondary colors:

Red + yellow = orange

Red + blue = purple

Blue + yellow = green

Color Blending

There are many fancy ways to create beautiful blends of colors. This very simple folding and rolling technique creates a blended sheet of clay.

Here's How:
1. Make three coils of three different colors.
2. Roll and flatten the colors together. Fold the flat sheet and roll again.
3. Repeat the folding and rolling until the colors have blended nicely. ❏

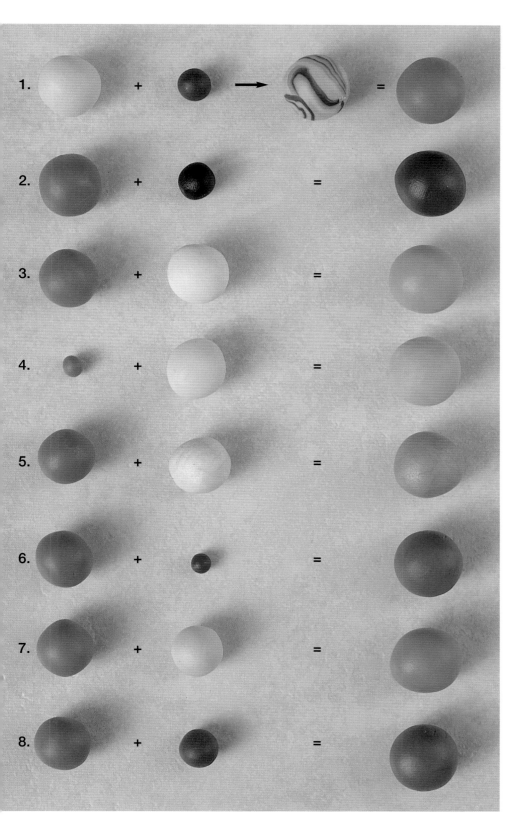

Color Mixing

This color chart shows some more color mixing. The color green was used as the example, but any primary or secondary color can be mixed the same way. Note the sizes of the clay balls. When mixing two colors, use more of the lighter color and a smaller amount of the darker color.

1. **Yellow + blue = green.** When two colors of clay are thoroughly mixed, the distinction between them disappears. However, if you stop the mixing part way, you'll get a marbled effect.

2. **Green + black = dark green.** Mixing black into a color makes a darker color.

3. **Green + white = light green.** Mixing white into a color makes a lighter color.

4. **Green + translucent = translucent green or ice green.** Mix only a very small amount of colored clay into translucent clay for ice colors. When baked, these colors change to soft, translucent hues.

5. **Green + pearl = pearl green.** Make any color a pearl color by mixing in pearl white.

6. **Green + red = muted green.** Mute (or make less intense) any color by adding its complement color (the color opposite it on the color wheel).

7. **Green + yellow = lime green.** By adding one of the adjacent colors on the color wheel, you create a new color.

8. **Green + blue = teal.** By adding the other adjacent color on the color wheel, you create yet another new color.

Basic Techniques

Here are the basic techniques used to make the projects in this book. All are simple and designed for young crafters.

Conditioning

Conditioning adds strength and smoothness and warms the clay for easier working. It's easier to condition a small amount of clay at a time. To condition, simply work with the clay in your hands until it reaches a softer consistency.

You can also roll clay to condition it. Cut the clay into slices and roll to flatten. Fold the flat sheet in half and roll again. Continue folding and rolling until clay is soft and pliable.

Wrap conditioned clay in wax paper and store in zip-top plastic bags away from bright light.

Making Clay Sheets

To make clay sheets, condition the clay well before rolling. Using a roller, go over the clay in different directions to make the clay sheet. Place wooden skewers along the sides to create a sheet with an even thickness (about 1/8").

Before you start, remember:
- Dirty fingerprints on light colors will ruin your results. Keep your hands clean, wiping them with hand wipes between colors.

- Use gentle, firm pressure to join pieces – it is not necessary to squash them together. They will fuse when baked.

Basic Clay Shapes

Here's How to make basic clay shapes:

1. **Ball** - Roll a small piece of clay in the palms of your hands until it is a round, smooth ball. TIP: If the ball is not round, you're probably pushing too hard.
2. **Flat ball** - Roll a ball and flatten into a circle.
3. **Teardrop** - Roll a ball, then roll on your work surface on one side until you have a sharp point.
4. **Coil** - Roll a piece of clay into a smooth ball. Shape the ball into a long log and place on your smooth work surface. With your fingers apart, roll the coil up and down until you reach the desired thickness. Use a light touch to make the coil an even thickness.

Making Simple Canes

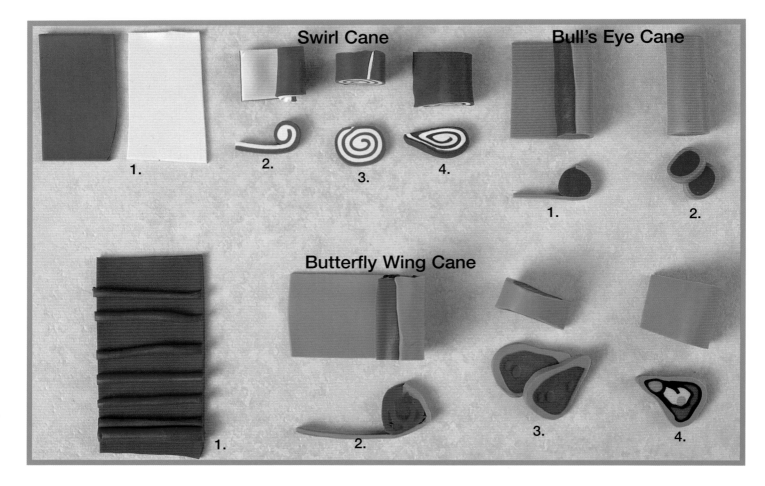

Canes are long coils of clay made of assembled smaller clay coils that are sliced to reveal their beautiful designs. You can make incredibly detailed canes, and you can roll them to create smaller diameter canes without spoiling the design. Here are some simple techniques:

Swirl Cane

Here's How:
1. Roll out two sheets of colored clay.
2. Place one sheet on top of the other and roll up like a jelly roll.
3. This is a slice of a round swirl cane.
4. You can shape the cane to alter the design. Here, I've pinched one edge to create a pointed swirl. ❏

Bull's Eye Cane

Here's How:
1. Make a coil of clay. Roll out a sheet of clay in another color. Place the coil on the flat sheet and roll together.
2. Trim the sheet when the coil is completely covered and smooth out the seam. The slices show the bull's eye cane. ❏

Butterfly Wing Cane

Here's How:
1. Roll out a sheet of clay. Place different colored coils on the sheet.
2. Roll up tightly. Cover the cane with another sheet of different colored clay.
3. Pinch the cane to create the wing shape.
4. Using different color combinations creates different effects. ❏

Layering for False Wood & Ivory

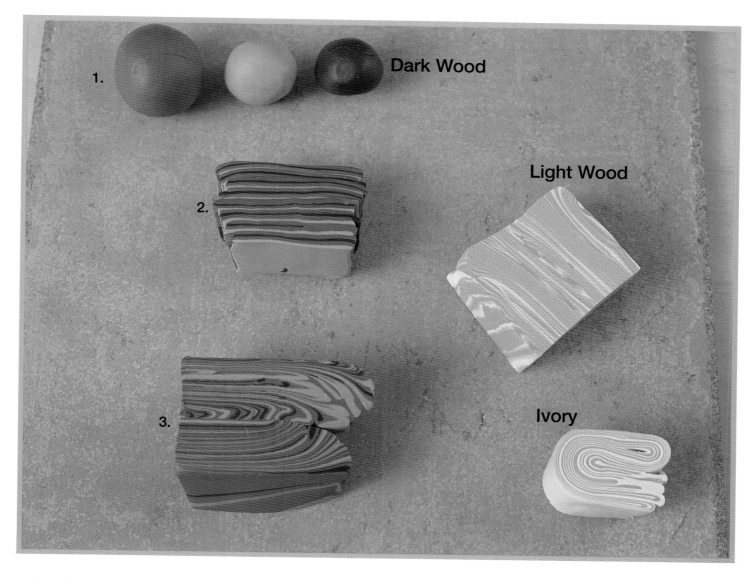

By rolling and folding different colors of clay, you can create the look of dark or light wood; I use the same techniques to make false ivory or bone.

Dark Wood

1. Start with three balls of clay: terra cotta, tan, and dark brown.
2. Roll the different colors of clay into thin sheets. Stack the flat sheets of the three colors. Fold this flat sheet in half and roll again. Continue folding and rolling until you have a multi-layered design that looks like the grain of wood.

3. Cut the layered stack. Place the pieces on top of each other until you have a stack 1-1/4" to 1-1/2" thick. Roll to fuse the stack into one piece. To create projects with false wood, cut a slice 1/4" thick and roll into a flat sheet. TIP: You can use the scraps to make "wooden" beads. ❏

Light Wood

Use white, tan, and beige clay balls.

False Ivory or Bone

Use white and transparent clay balls.

Covering Objects

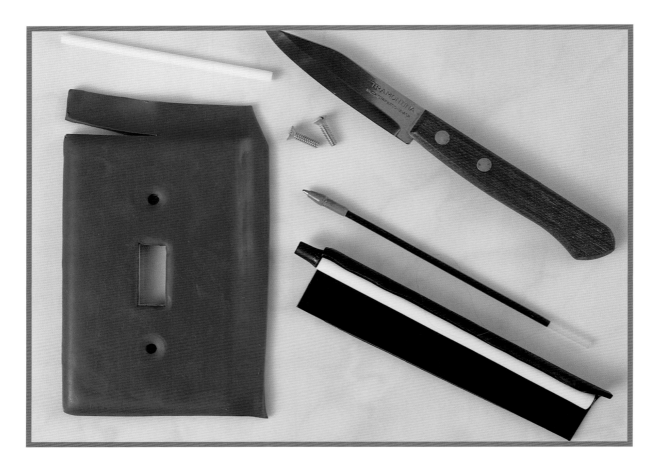

You can cover almost any object that will not melt in a 275 degree F. oven. This includes wood, cardboard, glass, metal, and many plastics. (*Always* test plastics first.)

Brushing the clay or the surface with white craft glue before applying the clay will help the clay bond.

Covering a Switch Plate

You can cover a switch plate with a thin sheet of clay and add decorative clay pieces to make a wonderful accent for your room. I prefer to use inexpensive plastic light switch plates. (You can also cover wooden or brass plates with polymer clay. If you use a new brass plate, be sure to remove the plastic coating first.)

Here's How:
1. Roll out well-conditioned clay to make a thin 4-1/2" x 6" sheet.
2. Brush white glue over the front of the switch plate.
3. Place the clay sheet over the plate and press to mold around the shape.
4. Use a knife to trim off the excess clay and cut the hole in the middle. Use a straw to create the holes for the screws.
5. Smooth all the edges with your fingers. Decorate with polymer clay shapes. ❏

Covering a Pen

It's easy and fun to make fantastic pens for your friends and family. Not all plastic pens will work as a base, some may melt. In my experience, pens with opaque plastic barrels work better than pens with clear barrels. There is no need to add glue to the barrel.

Here's How:
1. Remove the ink cartridge by twisting and pulling out the cartridge with a pair of pliers.
2. Roll and trim a thin sheet to 5" x 1-1/2". Wrap around the barrel of the pen. Trim off the excess clay from the top and bottom. Smooth the seam. ❏

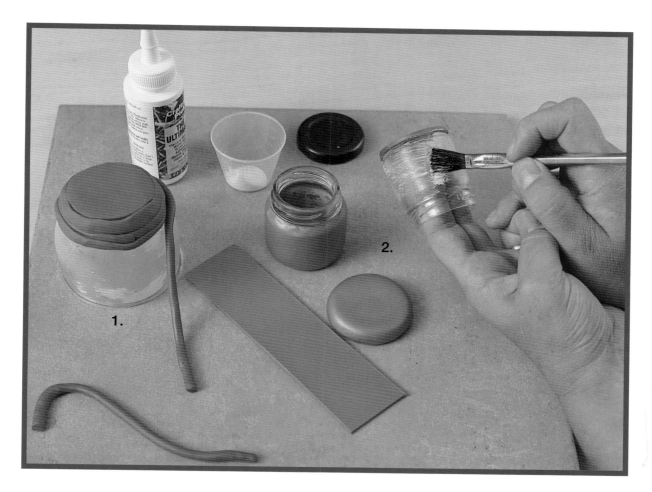

Here are two techniques that can be used to cover a variety of containers – glass jars and tins are two examples. Using an object under the clay is an easy way to make a container, and the finished project can hold water.

Technique #1 - The Coil Method

The coil method uses long coils of clay to cover an object. The coils can be curled, zigzagged, or wrapped over the base in a variety of ways.

Here's How:

1. Brush a layer of white craft glue all over the outside of the vessel.
2. Place a 1/8" thick sheet of clay on the bottom and trim around the base. (This creates the bottom.)
3. Roll a 10" long coil of clay about 1/4" thick. Starting at the bottom, wrap the coil around the vessel. Roll and wrap more coils until you reach the top. Don't worry about small spots left uncovered – they just add interest to the design.
4. When you are pleased with the coverage, press the coils together gently and smooth out any irregular areas. The coils can be left showing or completely smoothed away with your fingers. ❑

Technique #2 - Slab Method

This method of covering a vessel creates a very smooth surface that's perfect for stamping or decorating with texture tools. Use flat-sided jars, papier mache boxes, or tin cans as your base. In the photo, the lid was covered with a layer of glue and a thin piece of clay sheet to match the jar.

Here's How to cover the jar:

1. Brush a layer of white craft glue all over the outside of the vessel.
2. Place on a 1/8" thick sheet of clay on the bottom and trim around the base. (This creates the bottom.)
3. Measure the vessel height and circumference. Cut a piece to these measurements from a 1/8" thick clay sheet. (The recycled baby food jar here needed a piece of clay 1-1/2" x 6".)
4. Wrap this piece around the jar. Smooth out the seam, press the side and bottom pieces together, and mold the clay around the neck of the jar. If you're using a lid, don't cover the threads of the jar. ❑

Making Clay Bases

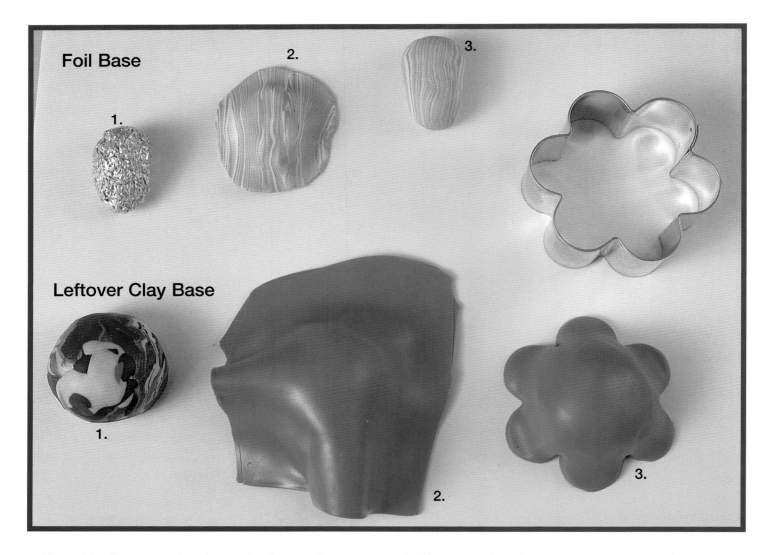

To avoid using so much polymer clay for a project, you can make a base and cover it with a sheet of clay. Here are instructions for making bases from aluminum foil and leftover bits of polymer clay.

Foil Base

Inexpensive household aluminum foil works well for when you want a lightweight base. (This example is a head for an African-style mask.)

1. Tightly crumple a piece of foil and form it into your desired shape. Make sure it is tightly packed and that the surface is smooth.
2. Roll and trim a sheet of clay to cover the foil base.

3. Wrap the clay sheet around the base, forming and smoothing the clay as you go. ❏

Leftover Clay Base

Use leftover clay when you want a heavier base for your project.

1. Form the leftover clay into the desired size and shape.
2. Roll and trim a sheet of clay to cover the base. Smooth and stretch the clay sheet over the edge and along the bottom edge base.
3. Trim the excess clay with a cookie cutter to add a decorative edge to the base. ❏

Making Eyes

When working with children, it's helpful to have a supply of pre-made eyes for projects. (Adults or older children can make them for younger children to use.) I prefer to make a tile full of eyes at a time. I bake them for 20 minutes at 275 degrees F. After they have cooled, they stick to the tile so they're ready to use when needed for a project.

Here's How to make basic eyes:

1. Roll a 1/4" coil of white clay. Mark and cut into 1/8" pieces.

2. Roll the white pieces into balls.

3. Flatten the balls into flat balls.

4. Roll a 1/8" coil of black clay. Mark and cut 1/16" pieces.

5. Roll the black pieces into balls. Position them on the white flat balls.

6. Flatten the black balls on the flattened white balls.

7. Roll a very tiny white coil. Cut into teeny, tiny pieces.

8. Roll these tiny pieces into tiny balls. Place one on each black flat ball at the top right. (These tiny balls are a bit tedious to make, but they add a sparkle to a character's eyes.) ❏

Other fun eyes to create include reptile eyes, alien eyes, and glow-in-the-dark eyes.

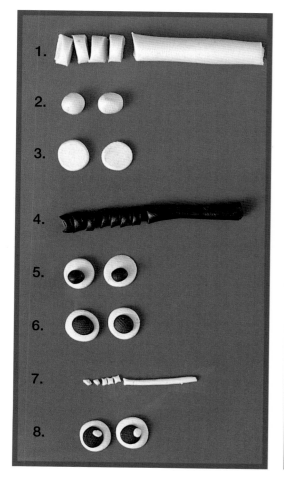

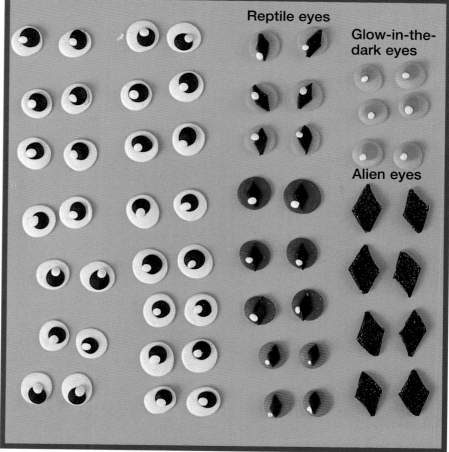

Reptile eyes

Glow-in-the-dark eyes

Alien eyes

Clay Mosaic Tiles

Making small polymer clay tiles for children to use in mosaic projects is fast and easy. There is no need to measure – slightly irregular tiles can add charm and interest to projects.

Here's How:
1. Roll out 1/8" thick clay sheets on a glazed tile.
2. Trim the sheets into 3" squares.
3. Using a paring knife, cut across the clay sheet at 1/4" intervals. Cut again at a 90 degree angle to create square tiles. (You can also cut diagonally to create triangular tiles.)
4. Bake the tiles for 20 minutes at 275 degrees F. When cool, the sheets easily break apart into approximately 100 square tiles. ❑

Using Clay to Attach Other Pieces

I've found it's best to use small pieces of clay to attach wire, cording, brooch backs, or other pieces to baked clay. The clay bonds well to the back of a piece without the use of specialty glues, many of which are unsafe to use with children. This method makes a strong, firm bond.

1. Bake the object you wish to bond to for 20 minutes at 275 degrees F. Let cool.
2. Turn the object over and, with a fresh piece of clay, attach the item to the back of the partially baked clay piece. Make sure you press the fresh clay down and out of the way of any mechanics such as a clasp or pin mechanism. (You could add a small layer of white craft glue for extra bonding power, but it is not usually necessary.)
3. Let children use alphabet stamps to stamp their initials into the clay to mark their pieces.
4. Bake again for the time and temperature specified in the project instructions. Let cool completely before picking up or moving. ❏

Baking the Clay

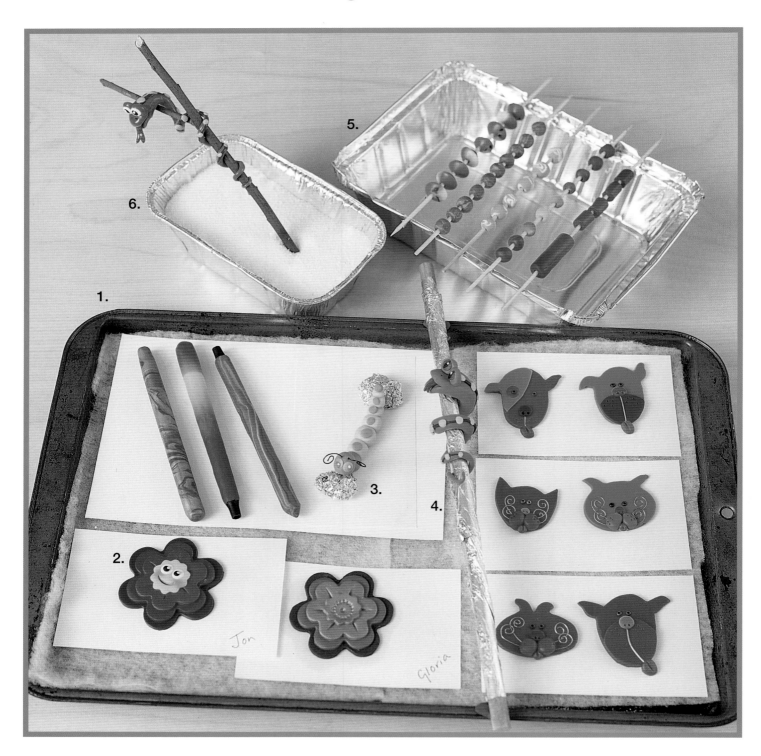

You can always just place the ceramic tile that was used as a work surface in the oven to hold projects while they bake. The smooth surface of the tile will make the back of the clay piece shiny.

When baking a large flat item, such as a frame, use this method to prevent warping. Place the finished item on a piece of card paper, and place the card paper on a ceramic tile. Carefully place another piece of card paper over the clay and then another ceramic tile, right side down. Bake for a little longer – the tiles insulate the clay. Do not remove the top tile until it is completely cool.

The photo on the previous page shows a variety of ways to bake different types of clay objects:

1. I like to use an old cookie sheet that will never be used again for food preparation for baking clay. I line the pan with a thin piece of polyester batting – this prevents the index cards holding the clay projects from sliding around during transport to the oven.

2. Regular card paper or index cards work well to bake projects on. Do not use dark colored cards – they can impart color to projects. Card paper does not leave a shiny mark on the clay, and you can write the child's name on the card to help him or her identify the project.

3. Use crumpled aluminum foil to support items with extended pieces when baking.

4. A foil wrapped dowel lets you bake objects, such as this twisting snake, that do not have a bottom to sit on.

5. Aluminum foil pans and wooden skewers are great for keeping beads round while baking. Cut slots into both sides of the foil pan. Slide the beads on wooden skewers and place them in the slots. (This setup is also great for letting beads dry after varnishing.)

6. An aluminum foil pan filled with sand holds a twig with a snake. (You can also use this pan to hold a project after varnishing.)

The main thing to remember when baking polymer clay is to not let your oven temperature get too high. If the clay gets hotter than 300 degrees F., it can burn and give off toxic fumes. Polymer clay normally gives off a slight odor when firing; this is nothing to worry about and not a sign that the clay is burning. To avoid burning, use an oven thermometer to double check the thermostat. Make sure the room is well ventilated – open windows and turn on the exhaust fan. If you do happen to burn a batch of clay, turn off the oven, leave the windows open and the fan on, and leave the house for an hour or two to give the toxic fumes time to clear.

BAKING TIPS

- Clay does not harden until it is completely cool.

- Clay that has not been baked long enough will be fragile and break easily.

- Some colors deepen when baked.

- Baking times are always estimates as there may be many sizes of projects being baked at the same time.

- Items can be re-baked several times without harm.

- You can bake longer, but never hotter! **Don't** raise the oven temperature!

- **Do not** use a microwave oven to bake polymer clay.

General Baking Guidelines

These are general guidelines. **Always** follow the manufacturer's recommendations for baking temperatures and times.

Most polymer clays - 15 minutes per 1/4" (5mm) of thickness at 275 degrees F. (130 degrees C.)

Flexible clays - 20 minutes per 1/4" of thickness (5mm) at 285 degrees F. (140 degrees C.)

Eraser Clays - 10 minutes *only* at 250 degrees F. (121 degrees C.) Eraser clay needs to be slightly underbaked to work as an eraser. If baked longer, it will not erase pencil marks.

After It's Baked

After polymer clay has been baked, you can drill it, sand it, varnish it, paint it, and/or glue it. The following pages show how.

Painting & Varnishing

Painting & Varnishing

It's easy to paint and varnish baked polymer clay. Wiping the clay item with rubbing alcohol before painting or varnishing helps the paint or varnish adhere to the clay.

Baked polymer clay should be painted with acrylic paints. **Do not** use oil-based paints – they will never dry properly.

Baked clay has a nice matte finish. There are a number of options for adding a shiny finish:

- For best results, use water-based polymer clay varnish made by polymer clay manufacturers.
- If you want to try another varnish, test it first. Be aware that other types of varnishes, such as spray finishes and nail polish, will react with the clay over time, causing it to turn sticky.
- Acrylic floor wax creates a nice, shiny finish. It is easy to use, dries quickly, and is very economical. In a large group, let children apply it with a cotton swab.

Follow this simple paint-and-sand technique to bring out imprinted textures or stamped designs. Steel wool sands the clay nicely, taking away the surface paint and leaving the details colored. Steel wool is easy for children to hold and works quickly, but it won't mar the piece if a child sands too much.

1. Bake the clay piece.
2. Brush on thinned acrylic paint.
3. If you wish, add more than one color.
4. Let the paint dry completely; then sand with a piece of steel wool. ❑

Gluing

The best glues for joining baked polymer clay pieces or for attaching jewelry findings are epoxy glues and "super" glues. Since both types are unsafe for children to use, I prefer to use clay pieces to attach these items when possible. See "Using Clay to Attach Other Pieces" for information about this technique.

Finishing Jewelry

Simply knotting the ends of necklace and bracelet cords finishes a piece of jewelry – I always add a touch of white craft glue to the cut ends to prevent unraveling.

Jewelry pieces also can be finished with a clay bead and a loop or crimp beads and a lobster clasp.

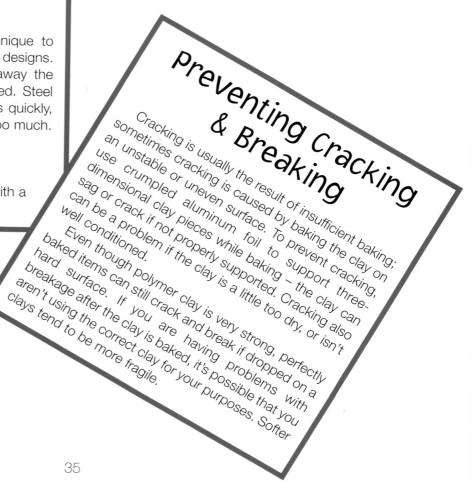

Preventing Cracking & Breaking

Cracking is usually the result of insufficient baking; sometimes cracking is caused by baking the clay on an unstable or uneven surface. To prevent cracking, use crumpled aluminum foil to support three-dimensional clay pieces while baking – the clay can sag or crack if not properly supported. Cracking also can be a problem if the clay is a little too dry, or isn't well conditioned.

Even though polymer clay is very strong, perfectly baked items can still crack and break if dropped on a hard surface. If you are having problems with breakage after the clay is baked, it's possible that you aren't using the correct clay for your purposes. Softer clays tend to be more fragile.

PROJECTS

This section includes ideas for crafting nifty tools to decorate your desk, trendy accessories to show off your talents, and beautiful gifts like jewelry, notebooks, and containers that will delight your family and friends. They are as much fun to make as they are to use!

Flower Face Bouquet

(Pictured on opposite page)

This cheerful bunch of blossoms is a perfect get-well gift or a memorable Mother's Day present. Choose a bouquet of silk flowers with large blossoms (ones with a center that's at least 1" in diameter). Pull off the flower heads. Attach a clay face to the center of each flower with white craft glue. (For instructions for making faces, see the next page.)

Set the blossoms in small paper cups while the glue dries. When they are completely dry, re-attach the flower heads to the wire stems. Wrap the stems in bright green tissue paper and tie with a colorful bow.

Funny Faces

These funny faces are simple so it's easy to make the animated expressions.

Many colors are used to create a rainbow of different faces.

Funny Faces

Look at all the different facial expressions you can create – exhausted, sad, sick, bratty, lovesick, happy, surprised. No doubt you'll think of more.

Here's how to make a basic face:
1. Roll a ball of clay and flatten to make a 1" flat ball.
2. Add the eyes. (For information on making eyes, see the Basic Techniques section.)
3. Cut a flattened 3/8" diameter ball in half for the eyelids.

Use a slightly darker color for the eyelids than what was used for the face.
4. Add the mouth with a smile tool (see the "Handmade Tools" section) or use a modeling tool. Add other features, if you like, such as a tongue or a teardrop.
5. Use a pink chalk pastel or powder blusher makeup to add a little blush on the cheeks.
6. Bake. ❑

Face Magnets

Simple Face Magnets

To make face magnets, simply glue a magnet to the back of a face.

Blooming Face Magnets

Blooming magnets frame the clay faces with flower petals. Remove the petals from the head of a silk flower. Arrange petals and glue together with white craft glue. Glue the face on top and Let dry. Add the magnet to the back.

Two-faced Lanyard

This makes a great zipper pull. You can also put one on a purse or hang one from a school binder as shown. Bake two faces made with contrasting colors. Take another ball of clay and squish the clay between the two baked faces. Make a wire loop and push it into the top of the soft clay. Bake again. Thread a piece of cord through the wire loop, thread beads over both of the cord ends, and tie to a metal lanyard to complete.

Notebooks, Cards & Bookmarks

Use a glue stick to glue paper panels together. To glue the clay face to card paper, use white craft glue.

Cards
1. Cut a 4" x 8" piece of colored card stock. Fold in half.
2. Cut 3-1/2", 3", 2-1/2", 2" square panels from brightly colored card stock. Trim the edges with decorative scissors.
3. Glue the panels to the card. Glue a face in the center. ❏

Bookmarks
Enclose these bright faces with a book and give as a gift.
1. Cut a 1-1/2" x 11" strip of card stock. Trim the ends with decorative edge scissors.
2. Cut 3", 2-1/2", and 2" square panels from brightly colored card stock. Trim the edges of the panels with decorative edge scissors. Glue them, one on top of the other, to the top of the long strip.
3. Glue a face at the center of the stacked paper squares. ❏

Three Faces Notebook
1. Cut a variety of colorful panels from card stock. Glue to the cover of a notebook.
2. Add faces. ❏

Cool Beads & Jewelry

You can make beads with polymer clay in a variety of shapes and just about any color. Use the beads to make the necklaces and bracelets or to decorate another project, like a lanyard to a keychain. Beadmaking instructions begin on the next page.

Bead Types & Techniques

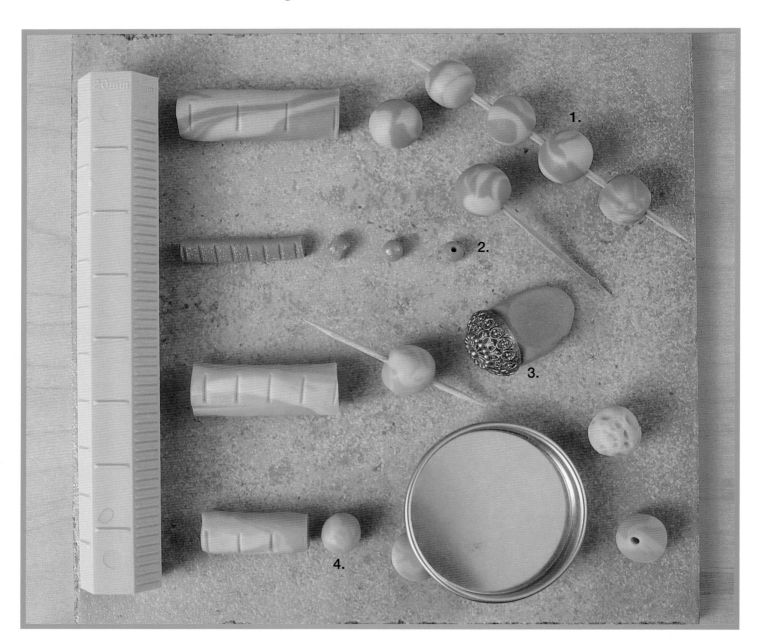

Type 1 - Basic Round Beads

Roll a coil of clay. (The size depends on the size of the bead.) Use a ruler to mark equal pieces. Cut off a piece and roll the clay in your hands to make a ball. Use a toothpick to pierce the hole. Thread the finished beads on a wooden skewer for baking.

Variation: To make **beads of graduated sizes**, mark the coil with a ruler to make equal-size pieces and cut. Make the first bead with one piece, the second bead with two pieces, the third bead with three pieces, and so on.

Type 2 - Sparkle Beads

Roll the coil for the beads in fine glitter before marking, cutting, and rolling into a ball.

Type 3 - Textured Beads

After rolling the clay in a ball and making the hole, leave the bead on the toothpick. Use a texture tool to imprint a design on the bead. Remove the toothpick and thread on a skewer.

Type 4 - Bicone Beads

These neat little beads are easy and fun to make. After making a round ball, roll the bead under a lid on a smooth surface so it looks like two cones joined together. Don't push too hard with the lid – just roll the bead around gently. Pierce the bead from one point to the other.

Type 5 - Tubular Beads

Roll out a thin piece of clay. Trim to make a flat strip 3/4" x 4". Roll the strip around a wooden skewer and smooth the seam. Mark the clay and cut into beads. (You can vary the length to make long or short tubes.) Clean up the ends with a modeling tool if necessary. Slide the beads apart slightly along the skewer before baking.

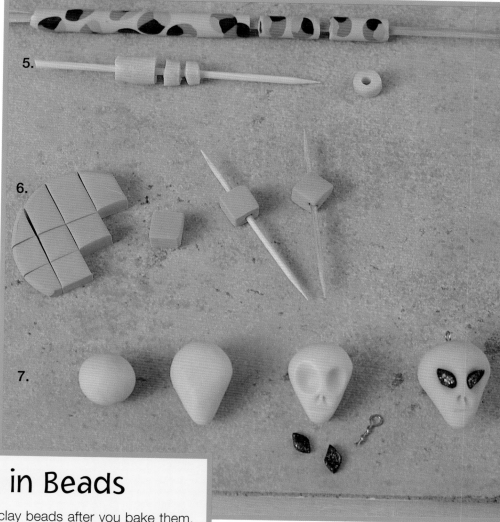

Making Holes in Beads

Though you can drill holes in polymer clay beads after you bake them, it's easier to make the holes *before* baking. It's also best to make the holes fairly large so threading the beads after baking is an easy task. Using this technique avoids deforming the bead and creating an unsightly lump around the edges of the hole.

1. Hold the bead between your fingers and poke a hole almost all the way through it with a round toothpick, letting the toothpick poke out slightly at the other end.
2. Withdraw the toothpick and poke it through from the other side, using the little mark as your guide. ❏

Type 6 - Square Beads

Roll out a 1/4" thick clay sheet. Use the knife to cut into squares. Smooth the sides. Pierce with a toothpick to make the hole.

Variation: Pierce the bead from corner to corner, creating a diamond-shaped bead.

Type 7 - Large Beads

I like to add wire loops to large beads for stringing rather than making holes in the beads. Form the bead shape. (This one is an alien head bead.) Using a modeling tool, add features and the black alien eyes with glitter. Make a wire loop to pierce the top by cutting a 2" piece of 20-gauge wire and twisting it around a wooden skewer. Trim the ends neatly and pull off the stick to create the wire loop. (This makes a very effective hanger for the bead; it will not pull out of the clay after baking.)

Heart & Bead Jewelry

Heart Pendants

1. Follow the instructions in the Basic Techniques section to make a heart tool.
2. Roll a small amount of clay into a ball.
3. Form the ball into a teardrop shape and flatten slightly.
4. Press the wide end of the shape into the point of the heart tool.
5. Form the bottom into a point. Add a wire loop to make a heart pendant. ❑

Ideas:

• Acrylic rhinestone gems can be glued to the hearts after baking. **Do not** attach rhinestones to raw clay – they cannot withstand the oven temperature.

• When creating a heart pendant necklace, be sure to make some matching beads.
• Mixing handmade polymer pendants and beads with smaller glass beads makes a beautiful piece of jewelry.

Glittery Bead Bracelet

1. Marble pink, purple, and blue "ice clay" (translucent clay mixed with very little colored clay).
2. Roll round beads.
3. Place the beads in a little plastic bag with some glitter and shake to coat evenly.
4. Make holes with a toothpick. ❑

44

Glow-in-the-Dark Space Beads

You can make lanyards, necklaces, and key rings or decorate surfaces with these beads. They're all made with glow-in-the-dark polymer clay.

- **Earth Beads** - Marble green and blue glow-in-the-dark clay together and form 1/2" diameter beads.

- **Moon Beads** - Marble orange and yellow glow-in-the-dark clay together and form 1/2" diameter beads. Use a texture tool to imprint the bead with craters.

- **Spaceship Beads** - Marble orange and green glow-in-the-dark clay together and form 1/2" bicone beads.

- **Spacer Beads** - Make small (1/4") blue glitter beads and 1/2" yellow glitter tube beads. Use them as spacers between larger beads.

- **Alien Head Beads** - See page 43 for instructions.

Glow-in-the-Dark Switch Plate

This practical plate will guide you in the dark.
1. Cover a plastic switch plate with a sheet of polymer clay.
2. Make various glow-in-the dark beads. Cut them in half and attach to the switchplate.
3. Add small clay star cutouts and flat balls of glow-in-the-dark clay. ❏

Animal Print Beads & Pencils

Animal print beads are a perfect project for older children. After baking, the beads can be fashioned into hemp chokers that are popular with both boys and girls.

Hemp string macrame chokers *pictured at right* are simple and inexpensive to make – they're made with a basic square knot around a base line. They don't take long to make, so be sure to have lots of hemp cord on hand. Be sure the bead holes are large enough to accommodate the thickness of four strands of hemp cord.

Fig. 1. - Leopard Beads
1. Make black, tan, and orange coils.
2. Place them together and roll to create a 1/4" thick cane.
3. Cut the tri-colored cane into 1/8" slices. Place on a 3/4" x 4" flat sheet of ivory clay.

4. With a roller, flatten the cane pieces into the clay sheet.
5. Wrap this piece around a skewer and smooth the seam.
6. Cut to form the beads. ❏

Fig 2. - Tiger Beads
1. Roll out uneven thin black strips to form the stripes.
2. Place on a 3/4" x 4" sheet of orange clay.
3. With a roller, flatten the strips into the clay sheet.
4. Wrap this piece around a skewer and smooth the seam.
5. Cut to form the beads. ❏

Fig 3. - Giraffe Beads
1. Create an orange and brown bull's eye cane and roll to a 1/4" thickness.
2. Cut the cane into 1/8" slices. Place on a 3/4" x 4" flat sheet of ivory clay.

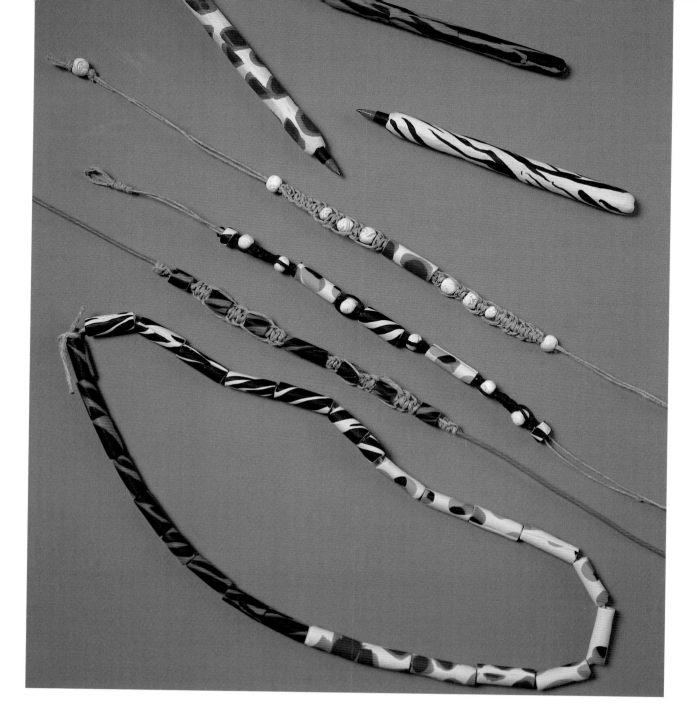

3. With a roller, flatten the cane pieces into the clay sheet.
4. Wrap the sheet around a skewer and smooth the seam.
5. Cut to form the beads. ❏

Fig. 4. - Zebra Beads
1. Roll out uneven thin black strips to form the stripes.
2. Place on a 3/4" x 4" flat sheet of white clay.
3. With a roller, flatten the strips into the clay sheet.
4. Wrap the sheet around a skewer and smooth the seam.
5. Cut to form the beads. ❏

Fig. 5.
A clay strip with cut beads on a wooden skewer.

Animal Print Pen
Use the animal print bead technique to make larger sheets to cover pens.
Here's How:
1. Roll out a clay sheet and trim 5" x 1-1/2".
2. Following the preceding instructions, create an animal sheet.
3. Cover a pen barrel with the sheet, smoothing the seam. ❏

Ideas for Pendants

Pendants can be used to make necklaces, bracelets, zipper pulls, and key chains. They use just a little clay and are easy for children to make. These pendants are about 3/4" x 1-1/4". Try different colors and color washes to create a variety of different stone finishes.

Here's How:
1. Make a ball of clay 3/4" in diameter.
2. Flatten the ball slightly and form into a teardrop shape.
3. Press the clay on a rubber stamp or use a handmade wire tool to create an imprinted design.
4. Pierce the top with a toothpick to form the hole.
5. Bake, then paint and sand to show off the design. ❏

Variation A: False carved ivory. See the Basic Techniques section for how to make ivory.

Variation B: False carved jade. Make jade by marbling together green, gray, and translucent clays.

Cookie Cutter Fun

Use cookie cutters to make decorative shapes with polymer clay.
You can use these decorative shapes to cover items or to make pieces
of jewelry as shown in the photos.

How to Make Flower:

1. Roll out a yellow clay sheet. Cut out the flower center, using a cookie cutter.
2. Place the yellow center on a red clay sheet. Cut out the flower.
3. Place the flower on a black clay sheet. Using a slightly larger flower-shaped cutter, create the black border around the blossom.
4. Imprint the yellow center with a button texture tool, and add petal details with a modeling tool.

Variation: Make templates from card paper and cut around them to create the shapes.

How to Make Leaf:

1. Use a crimped circle cutter and overlap cuts to form the leaf shape.
2. Place the leaf on a black sheet. Cut again, leaving the black border.
3. Add the veins, using a modeling tool.

Scissors Variation: Cut out the leaf shape with decorative edge scissors. ❑

Flowers and leaves can be made into magnets (here, they decorate a metal pencil cup), a flower and leaf necklace, and a bright and cheerful switch plate. The bee's body was cut in half to lay flush to the blue clay-covered plate.

Funky Flower Photo Holder

A photo holder makes a great gift. Use 18 gauge plastic coated wire for best results. The wire stems are 5" inches long and have coiled ends to hold photos.

Here's How to Make the Three-Flower Version:

1. Create three flowers and three leaves using the cookie cutter technique. Bake.

2. Cut three pieces of wire and coil one end of each piece to hold a photo. Add a wire piece to the back of each flower with a fresh piece of clay and bake again to bond the wires to the flowers. Set the finished flowers aside.

3. To make the base, make a 2" diameter ball of leftover clay. Cover with a 6" square green clay sheet. Add ladybugs to the base. (See page 58 for ladybug instructions.)

4. Push the wire ends of the flowers and leaves in the base. Bake the whole assembly to finish.

Variation: A single flower with two leaves at the base can make a cheery photo holder or memo holder.
❏

Pictured left to right: Single Flower Photo Holder or Memo Holder; Three-Flower Photo Holder.

Cookie Cutter Hearts & Stars

Other examples of cookie cutter creations *(pictured clockwise from top left)* include a Rainbow Star Key Chain and a Rainbow Star Necklace. Use the simple color blending technique to make the rainbow-colored sheet of clay.

The Sleepy Star Magnet was cut from a rainbow clay sheet; a sleepy face and mini stars were cut from the sheet trimmings.

The Heart Pin *at left* shows a lovesick face with mini heart accents. Use decorative edge scissors to cut a frilly border around the heart face on the Sweetheart Lanyard, *above.*

Kitty Whiskers & Panting Pooch

These whimsical animal heads are made with card paper templates – place them on clay sheets and cut around them to create the shapes. (See the back of the book for patterns.) Using bright clay colors adds to the fun look. Fashion these charming creatures into magnets, pins, and necklaces.

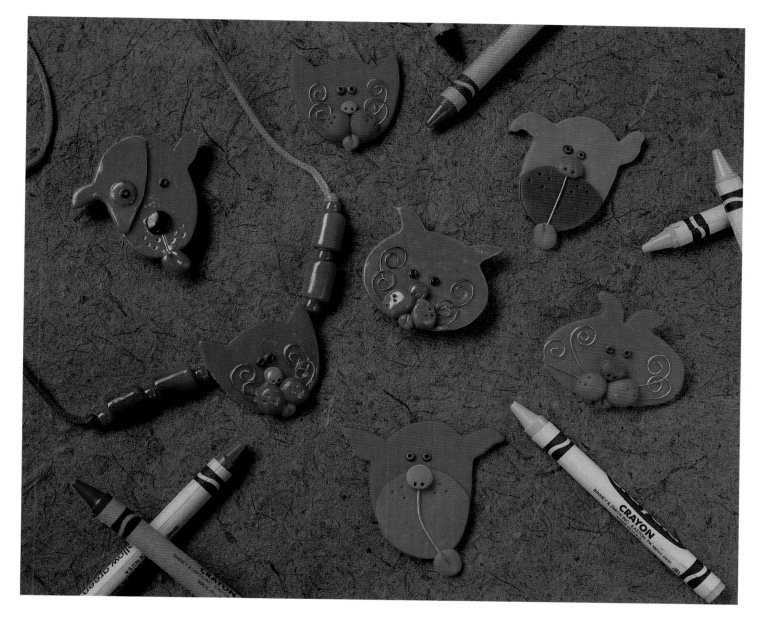

Kitty Whiskers

Here's How:
1. Cut out the templates from card paper, using the pattern. Place the template on a clay sheet and cut out with a knife.
2. Add a small clay ball for the kitty's nose. Using 22-gauge wire, make four curled wire pieces. Push them into the clay for the whiskers.
3. Add two glass seed beads for eyes, two balls of clay for a muzzle, and a small red ball for the tongue. Use a toothpick to add nostrils and details on the muzzle. Use a modeling tool for the tongue detail. ❏

Panting Pooch

Here's How:
1. Cut out the templates from card paper, using the patterns. Place templates on different-colored clay sheets and cut out with a knife.
2. Place the muzzle on the head. Add a small (1") piece of 20-gauge wire.
3. Add two glass seed beads for eyes, a small ball for the nose, and a small red ball for the tongue. Use a toothpick to add nostrils and details on the muzzle. Use a modeling tool for the tongue detail. ❏

Bookmarks

To make bookmarks, flexible clay is rolled into sheets 1/8" thick. Use templates to cut the pieces, then place them together like a puzzle and smooth the seams to bond the pieces together. Flexible clay is very soft and bonds together well, and thin pieces made from it won't crack and break. See the back of the book for patterns.

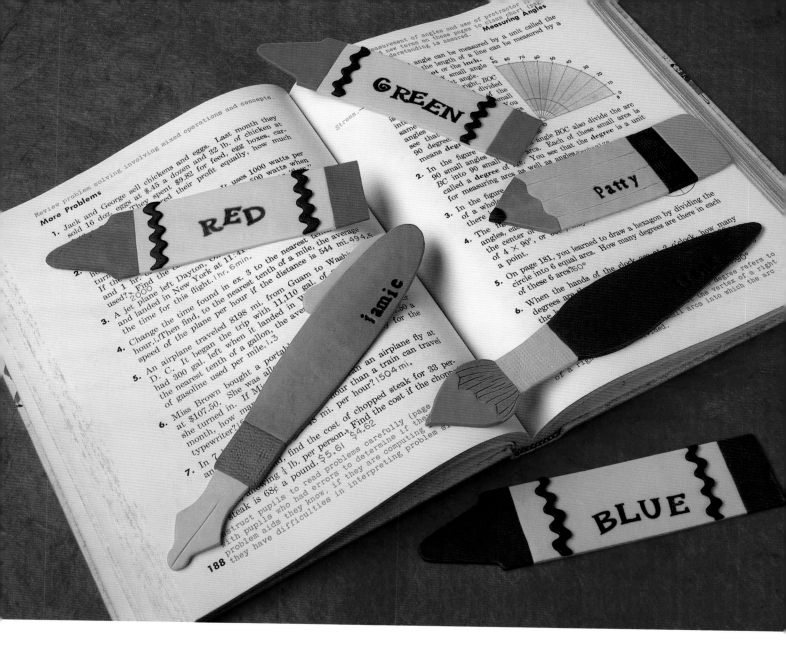

Crayon Bookmarks

Here's How:

1. Cut out the templates from card paper. Place the templates on colored clay sheets and cut out, using a paring knife.

2. Lay the pieces together on a tile and smooth the seams to join.

3. Add details, such as the zigzag piece for the crayon label. It's cut from a black clay sheet with decorative scissors. Use a texture tool and a modeling tool to add details on the other pieces.

4. With alphabet stamps and a black ink stamp pad, stamp the color of the crayon, your name, or your school's name. Do not attempt to remove the crayon from the tile – simply place the tile in the oven and bake to harden. ❏

Pictured above: The Paint Brush, Fountain Pen, Pencil, and Crayons Bookmarks also make great magnets for decorating a school locker. See back of the book for patterns.

Itty Bitty Bugs

These bright little bugs are perfect adornments for paper clips, bulletin board tacks, pens, and paperweights. The dragonflies and butterflies can clip on indoor plants or desk lamps to add a colorful accent. The wire antennae are optional – usually I leave them off bugs used for push pins or tacks to avoid getting poked in the finger with the wire ends.

Beetle with a Cane Design

Here's How:

1. Roll out a sheet of fuchsia clay and trim to 2" x 4". Roll three dark purple coils and place on the trimmed sheet.
2. Roll up the clay tightly. Wrap with 2" x 4" sheet of yellow clay. Roll to make a cane 1/2" thick. Cut into slices 1/8" thick.
3. Make a 1/2" diameter green ball and flatten slightly for the body.
4. Cut the cane slice in half and place on the green body.
5. Add a 1/4" diameter ball for the head. Add eyes with a toothpick. *Option:* Add tiny antennae with 22-gauge wire.
6. Bake. You can glue the beetle on a push pin (TIP: Some push pins melt, so it is better to have an adult glue it on after it is baked with a strong gel glue) *or* attach the beetle to a paper clip with a fresh piece of clay and bake again. ❑

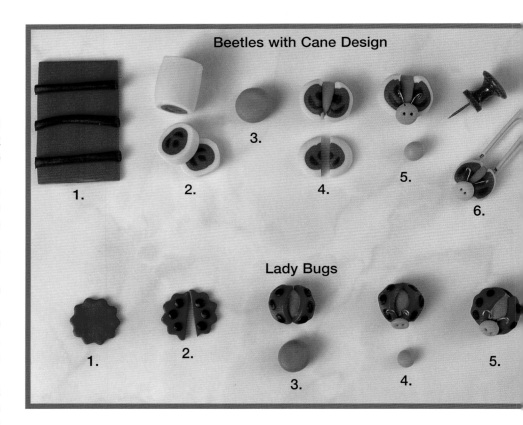

Beetles with Cane Design

1. 2. 3. 4. 5. 6.

Lady Bugs

1. 2. 3. 4. 5.

Lucky Ladybugs

Here's How:

1. Cut a circle from a red sheet of clay with a small crimp-edge cookie cutter.
2. Cut this piece in half. Add tiny flattened black clay balls to create the dots.
3. Make the green body with a 1/2" diameter ball and flatten slightly. Place the red and black body pieces around the green piece.
4. Add a 1/4" green ball for the head. Add eyes with a toothpick. *Option:* Add tiny antennae with 22-gauge wire.
5. Glue the finished ladybug to a magnet. ❑

The large Ladybug Paperweight was created on a 2" diameter base of leftover clay. The base was covered with a green clay sheet and texture was added with the modeling tool. Large flattened black balls create the dots and are accented further with cutout heart shapes. You can also use ladybugs to decorate paper clips, magnets, or a covered pen.

Beetle Paperweight & Memo Clip

These projects were made with a 2" diameter ball of leftover clay covered with a green clay sheet and decorated with small beetles. The "flying beetle" was baked on a wire before it was pushed in the clay base.

Here's How:
1. Cut a circle from the green clay sheet with a cookie cutter and drape over the clay ball.
2. Place on a sheet of purple clay and trim with a slightly larger cutter.
3. Push the oversized paper clip in the clay base and decorate the base with beetles. Add the flying beetle on a piece of 18-gauge wire. Bake. ❑

Call
Kevin
about project!

Stuff
4 project:
colored paper
markers
glue

Butterflies & Dragonflies

You'll see how to make dragonflies on the following page. Two variations on Dragonfly Clothespins are pictured here. They are made the same way, but the green and red ones use the butterfly wing cane to make the wings. See the Basic Techniques on page 24 for instructions for making butterfly wing canes.

The Butterfly Jar is a glass jar decorated with a butterfly – use white craft glue to attach the raw pieces of the butterfly to the jar before baking. The lid is covered with slices of the cane used for the butterfly wings.

The caterpillars and a glowworm (made with glow-in-the-dark clay) have dragonfly-style bodies. They are butterflies that have not yet grown their wings!

Bees & Dragonflies

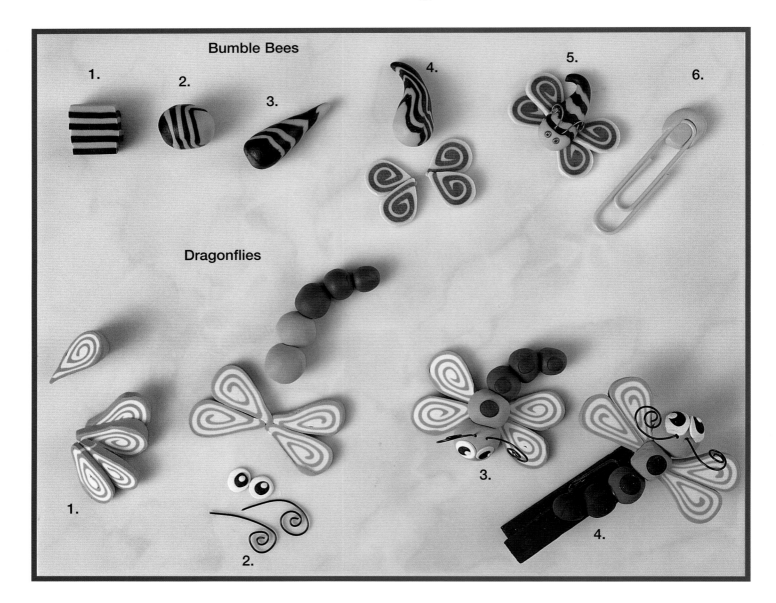

Dragonflies

Here's How:

1. Make a spiral cane with white and turquoise clay. Cut four slices for the wings.
2. To make the body, roll five balls in graduated sizes. Make the largest (the head) about 1/2" in diameter and the smallest 3/8" in diameter.
3. Arrange the wings. Press the body on top. Add the eyes, wire antennae, and flattened purple balls on the body segments.
4. Bake. Glue to a painted clothespin. ❑

Bumble Bees

Here's How:

1. Stack small sheets of yellow and black clay and cut into 1/2" squares.
2. Form the stack into a ball.
3. Form the ball into a teardrop shape.
4. To make the wings, cut four slices of a white and gold spiral cane.

5. Arrange the wing slices and push the body piece on top. Add gold seed beads for the eyes and curly wire antennae.
6. Put a piece of clay underneath a paper clip and press the bee in place on top. Bake. ❑

Pictured above: Bumblebees are used to decorate paper clips, a push pin, and a covered pen.

Clay Mosaics

Making mosaic items with polymer clay is a wonderful project for younger children – it stimulates their creativity and helps develop fine motor skills.

Making the little tiles ahead of time and using well-conditioned or softer clay for the base make the mosaic process easy. You can make lots of tiles with very little clay – almost 500 1/4" tiles can be made from a 2-oz. clay block – so mosaics are economical to do with a large group.

Here's How:

1. Cut out a base shape from a 1/4" thick clay sheet, using a cookie cutter or a card template and a paring knife.
2. Use sandpaper in an up-and-down motion (NOT back-and-forth) to add texture to the shape.
3. Press baked clay tiles and beads to the base to create the mosaic.
4. Bake the finished mosaic piece. ❑

Southwestern Style Mosaics

Colorful mosaic tiles decorate terra cotta bases to make picture frames, boxes, and keychains for that southwest flair. Instructions for these projects begin on page 66.

Southwestern Style Mosaics

These southwestern style mosaic projects use soft terra cotta colored clay for their bases. (The clay is available in 1.75 lb., 8 lb., and 24 lb. packages.) Make a selection of gold, brick red, black, aqua (green turquoise), blue turquoise, and copper tiles. The black, gold, copper, and green turquoise colors come right out of a package. I mixed the other two colors as follows:

Blue turquoise - Green turquoise + blue
Brick red - Red + a little brown

Decorate the terra cotta bases with tiles to make picture frames, boxes, keychains, and all kinds of decorative shapes.

Tile-topped Box

Here's How:
1. Cover the top of a round papier mache box with a sheet of 1/4" thick terra cotta clay.
2. Smooth the clay and add texture with sandpaper.
3. Decorate the top with small tiles and bake.
4. Paint the bottom of the box with turquoise acrylic paint.
5. Varnish with glossy acrylic varnish. ❑

Heart Keychain

Here's How:
1. Use clay in the tile colors to make coordinating beads.
2. Cut a heart from a clay sheet.
3. Decorate with tiles and tiny silver beads.
4. Place a wire loop in the top of the heart for the hanger. ❑

Moon & Star Magnets

Beads and metallic mosaic tiles decorate these magnets. After baking the decorated base, simply glue magnetic strips on the back.

Mosaic Frames

Here's How:
1. Make a card paper template the size of your desired frame, using shape templates (find them at crafts stores) to cut the frame openings.
2. Place a 1/4" thick sheet of the base clay on a ceramic tile and use the paper template to cut out the frame.
3. Add texture to the surface with a piece of sandpaper.
4. Position the tiles on the frame.
   • It's not necessary to completely cover the frame – you can create interesting designs and leave some areas of the frame plain.
   • Personalize your frame with alphabet rubber stamps – use a black inkpad to stamp your name, the date, or a favorite saying.
5. Place a piece of card paper on the frame. Place another tile on top of the paper. Bake the frame "sandwiched" between the tiles to prevent it from warping.
6. Cut a piece of mat board slightly smaller than the outside dimensions of the frame. Position a photograph on the mat board and glue to the back. (Silicone-based glue works best for attaching the mat board, but white craft glue also could be used.)
7. Fashion a stand by cutting a piece of mat board 2" x 4" and taping to the back with strong tape. (The tape acts like a hinge so the stand can lay flat or be adjusted to prop up the frame.) ❑

Glow-in-the-Dark Mosaics

Tiles made from glow-in-the-dark clay look great on black backgrounds.
Mosaic light switch plates and keychains are fun, practical gifts.

Clay Erasers

Eraser clay is especially fun for children to work with – it's very soft and requires little conditioning. When properly baked (for only 10 minutes at 250 degrees F. (121 degrees C.)), the clay will rub away pencil marks just like an eraser does. (If you overbake it, the clay will be too hard to erase.)

Ice Cream Cone Eraser

A simple-to-make 3" cane will make six ice cream cone erasers for friends. Children love the magic of cutting slices from a cane.

Here's How:
1. Make a 3" long tan brown coil that is 3/4" thick, using equal amounts white, brown, and orange eraser clay. Form the coil into a cone shape.
2. Make two white and pink marbled coils, each 3" long and 1/2" in diameter. Flatten the coils.
3. Make a pink and white marbled coil 3" long and 1/2" diameter. For the cherry, make a pink coil 3" long and 1/8" thick.
4. Layer all the pieces and squish together to form the ice cream cone cane. Cut slices 1/2" thick to form the erasers. TIP: If the cane is too soft to slice, place it in the refrigerator for 10 minutes to harden slightly, then slice. Add details on the cone with modeling tool before baking. ❏

Sandwich Eraser

Here's How:
1. From a 1/4" thick white eraser clay sheet, cut two 1-1/2" squares. (These are the slices of bread.) Brush brown chalk on the edges to make the crust.
2. For the sandwich fillings, make a 1" round pink circle for the tomato, a 1" crimped brown circle for the meat, a 1" square piece of orange for the cheese, and a hand-formed (irregular) 1-1/4" green circle for the lettuce.

3. Stack all the fillings between the bread slices and squish together – make sure they are stuck together well. Use a texture tool on both sides of the bread. Cut the sandwich in half and bake. ❑

Rainbows on Pencils

Layer different colored sheets of eraser clay around a coil to create a rainbow cane – start with a coil of red and bend the sheets around it to create the rainbow shape. Slice the rainbows. Push on the end of a pencil and bake. ❑

Eraser Orbs

These are fun to make. They slowly reveal different colors as the eraser is used.
1. Wrap a ball of marbled clay with a plain, colored clay sheet. Smooth all the bumps.
2. Add contrasting colored dots or coils to decorate. ❑

Earth Eraser

Wrap a clay ball with a blue clay sheet (for water). Smooth and add cutouts from a green sheet (for land) and cutouts from a white sheet (for polar ice caps). The layers will vanish as the eraser is used. ❑

More clay erasers! Using the same techniques, you can create a hamburger eraser or a hot dog eraser. You can also create planets, decorated orbs, and rainbows.

Sticky Notebooks

Another type of specialty clay can be used to make flexible hinges for notebooks. Flexible polymer clay can be used for the book covers as well as the flexible hinge or just used for the hinge with regular clay used for the covers. The examples on the following pages show a variety of hinge shapes. The flexible clay hinges allow the books to be opened and closed without cracking or breaking.

For the notebook pages, choose square or rectangular sticky note pads (readily available at office supply, stationery, drug, and grocery stores) or the newer die-cut sticky note pads that come in a variety of shapes. You can easily vary the number of pages in each book by dividing the note pads.

Here's How:

1. Roll out two sheets of clay bigger than the size of the note pad. Using a page from the note pad as a pattern, cut out two shapes from the flat sheets. (These are the notebook covers.)

2. Cut out decorative details from clay sheets with cookie cutters. Use the shapes to decorate the front cover.

3. Stack pieces of mat board to create a pile the same height as the sticky note pad. Cover the stack with foil. (This will hold the book cover in place while baking.)

4. To assemble the book cover for baking, stack the bottom cover, the foil covered mat board stack, and the top cover. A green leaf cut

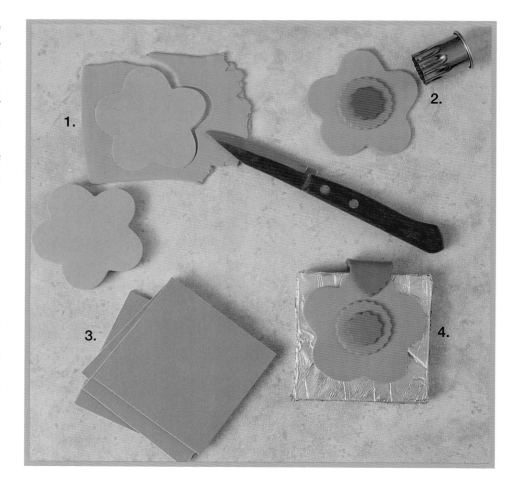

from flexible clay is the hinge. Wrap it around the stack, connecting the front and back covers. Press the leaf against the covers slightly to ensure a good bond. Bake. After the piece is cooled, remove the mat board stack and replace it with the sticky note pad, attaching the note pad with a little white craft glue. ❏

Flower & Leaf notebooks

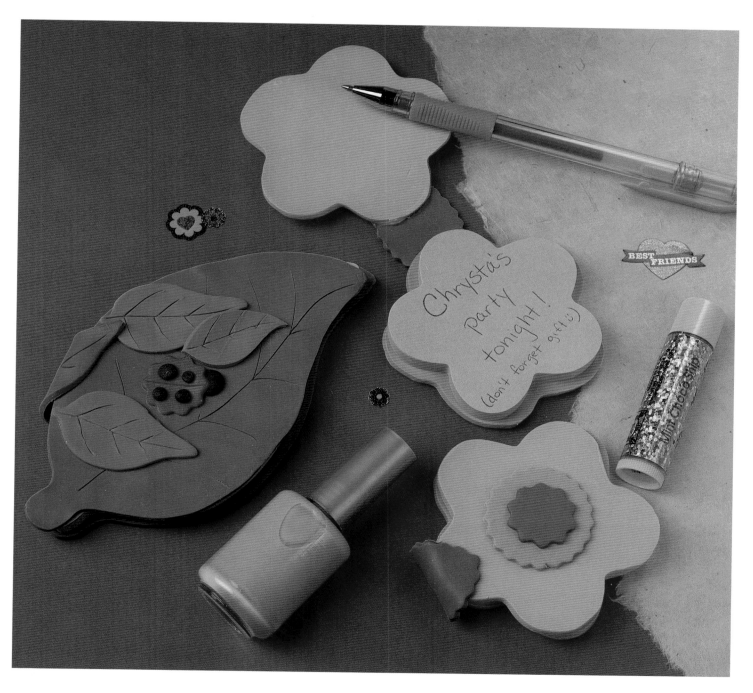

These fun little notebooks are made with die-cut sticky note pads. A little ladybug and extra leaves are added to the leaf book for added interest.

Tooled False Leather Notebook

The covers of this notebook are made of regular polymer clay, and the black hinge pieces are made of flexible clay. The front cover is decorated with eraser stamps (see the Basic Techniques section), painted, and sanded to give the look of tooled leather. A square sticky note pad is used for the pages. A clay button strung with gold elastic cord helps hold the notebook together.

Star Notebook

This notebook's covers are made of regular polymer clay.
The long hinge piece is made with flexible clay. Stars made of
glow-in-the-dark clay decorate the cover.

Marbled Magic Wands

These enchanting wands are a great craft project for your next wizard party. Don't forget to add a little magic while making them!

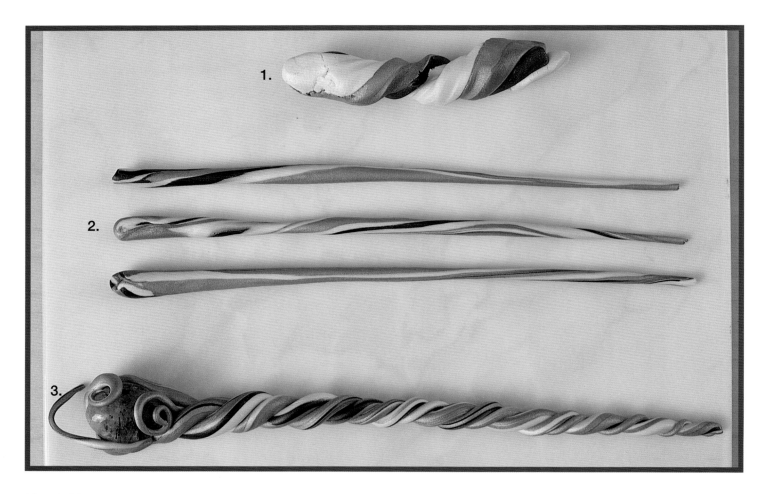

Here's How:
1. Marble three colors together.
2. Form three coils, slightly tapered. Make the coils about 8" long for a medium-size wand.
3. Twist or braid the coils to form the wand. Place a polished stone in a coordinating color into clay at the top thick end. Use small coils to form curving pieces to hold the stone firmly in place. Bake to harden.

Color Combinations For Wands:
• *Light Blue, Purple & Fuchsia Wand* - Glow-in-the-dark light blue, dark purple, and fuchsia coils are twisted together and rolled slightly. A flat clear marble is used at the top. TIP: Don't let the children know they are using glow-in-the-dark clay. After the wand is made, you turn off the lights for a magical surprise.

• *Ice Wand* - Mix transparent clay with small amounts of green, blue, and purple clay to make ice colors. Marble the ice colors with transparent clay. Twist three coils together and bake for a semi-translucent effect.

• *Blue, Yellow & White Twisted Wand*

- *Black, White & Silver Wand -* Varnish this one for a shiny finish.

- *Pink, Blue, & Purple Ice Wand -* Braid the coils for a different look.

Critters

Frogs, lizards, and snakes can decorate clay covered pens, be used as magnets, hang off twigs for plant pokes, and adorn clay pots or light switch covers. Or just keep one on your desk to keep you company. When you've learned to make the frog, it's easy to create the lizard and the snake.

Frogs

Here's How:

1. Form a light green coil about 2" long. Flatten and shape to make the belly piece. Make a green body about 2-1/2" long. Decorate with colorful dots of clay.

2. Add the light green belly piece to the bottom of the green body piece and smooth. Make four teardrop-shaped pieces for the upper legs. Decorate these pieces with colorful dots and position on the body. Position the body with the head off the surface. If you are making the frog on a pot or twig, use a little white glue to make a strong bond.

3. Make four teardrop shapes for the flippers and flatten the large end. Use a knife to cut out the "toes." End each with a colorful flat ball of clay. Press in place.

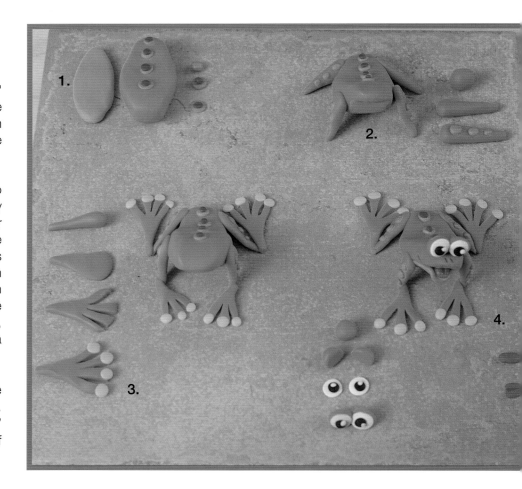

4. To make the mouth, cut and open the top part of the body. Make a small ball of clay the same color as the body, cut it in half, and position it above the mouth. Add the eyes and a tongue. ❏

The various bright, fluorescent colors make these creations dazzling and joyful; try flexible clay or glow-in-the-dark clay for special effects. A book with colorful tropical frogs is a great inspiration for the children when creating.

Even though I made my frogs green, they come in many different bright colors! Pre-making the eyes makes this project easier for younger children; older children will want to make their own eyes. Basic eyes – like the ones on the frog on the right – give a more comic appearance; reptile eyes – like the ones on the frog at left – give a more realistic look.

For tadpoles, make little, fat teardrop-shaped coils and add eyes.

Snakes & Lizards

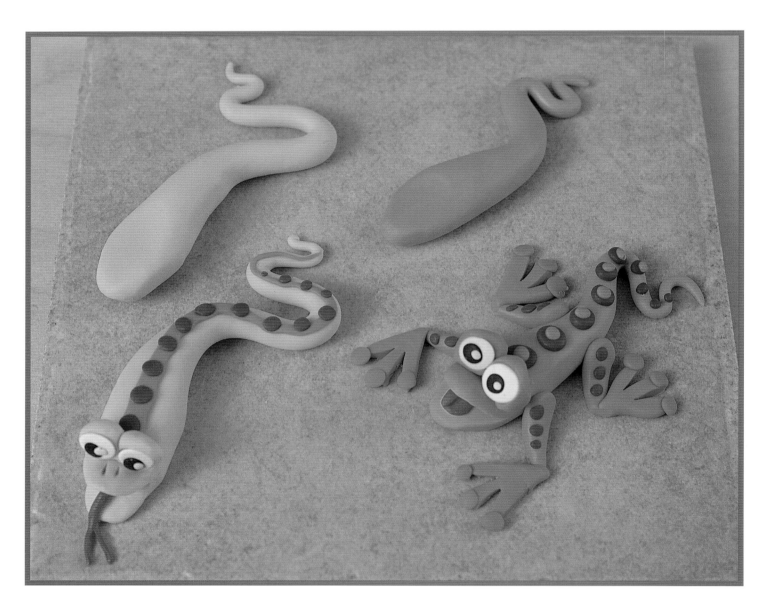

Snake

The snake is the simplest creature to make! Roll out a tapered coil body. Decorate with thinner coils and colorful dots of clay. Make the snake's head the same way as the frog's, but give the snake a forked tongue.

Lizard

To make a lizard, start with a tapered coil snake-like body; then follow the instructions for making a frog.

Critter Projects

Use a variety of colors when creating critters – you can make them any size you like. The jumping frog magnet's teardrop-shaped legs were formed around a wooden toothpick and then poked into the body piece. Using the toothpick pieces prevents the long limbs from breaking off.

The little snake perched on the rock is made with marbled green clay. (The rock is made of clay, too – see the Saying Stone project instructions on page 87 to learn how to make it.)

Froggy Frames

These frames have been textured with a rock, painted, and sanded after baking to create the stone-like appearance. The glossy varnished frogs show up nicely against this rustic background. You can also imprint frames with leaves, design stamps, rubber stamps, and home-made texture tools. Basic step-by-step instructions for making frames appear on the following pages.

These critters are made and baked right on the twigs, clay pots, light switch plates, pens, and frames. The coiled green snake was formed around a foil-covered dowel with flexible clay. (Using flexible clay allows you to wrap the snake on plant stems – or even around your finger – without breaking.)

Picture Frames

Picture frames are a great gift idea for children to make. Make sure the clay is conditioned well before rolling.

Here's How:

1. Cut the size of your desired frame from card paper. Position and cut out the frame window. (A shape cutter and templates – available in craft stores – makes this easy.) Place a sheet of 1/4" clay on a ceramic tile. Place the paper template on top. Cut out with a paring knife.

2. To prevent texture and design tools from sticking to the clay, brush the frame with cornstarch.

3. Decorate your frame. Here are some ideas:
   • To make a hanging frame, use a small plastic straw to make holes.
   • Personalize your frame using alphabet rubber stamps and a black inkpad to stamp your name, a special date, or a favorite saying.

4. Bake the frame on the tile with another piece of card paper and a tile on top to prevent the frame from warping.

5. Cut a piece of mat board slightly smaller than the frame. Position a photograph on the mat board and glue to the back of the frame. (Silicone-based glue works best, but white craft glue also can be used.)

6. Cut a piece of mat board 2" x 4" for a stand and tape to the back with strong tape. The tape acts like a hinge so the stand can lay flat or prop up the frame. ❏

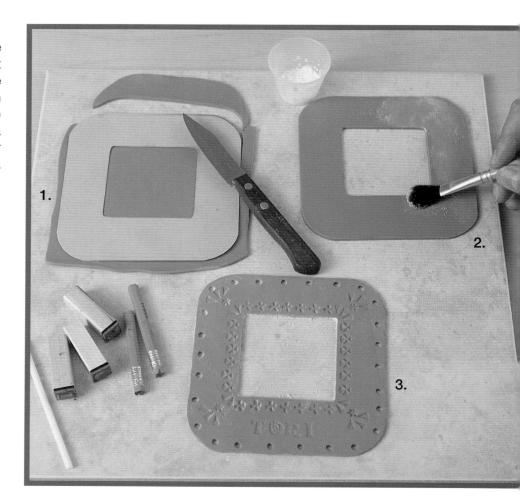

Leaf Frame

Fresh leaves were pressed into a clay frame with a roller to impart the leaf pattern and details. Use a plastic straw to make the five holes along the top of the frame. After baking, paint and sand the leaves to bring out the details. Tie a twig to the top with a piece of jute threaded through the holes. Knot the jute at the top to create the hanger.

Covered Pens

Covered pens make great gifts. You can make stands to hold the pens with the pen cap. Remember to remove the ink tube from the pen before covering and baking.

Feathered Bird Pen

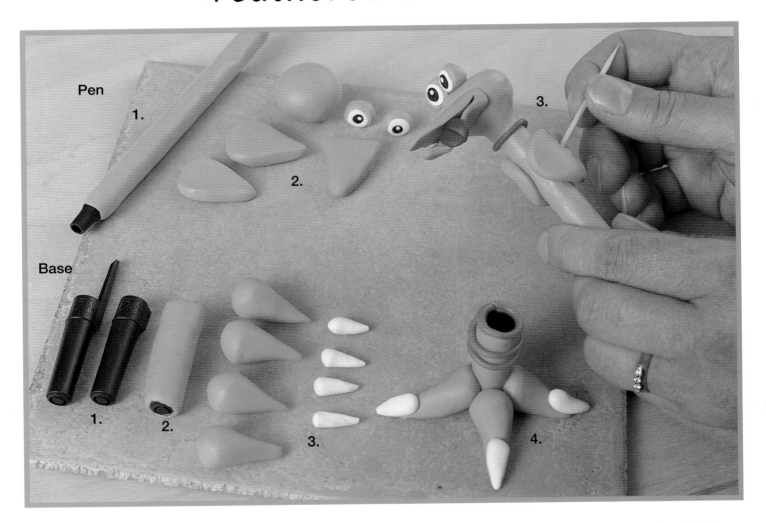

Here's How to Make the Pen:

1. Cover a pen barrel with a green clay sheet and smooth the seam.
2. Make a 1" green ball for the head and two 1-1/2" long wing shapes from green clay. Make a 3/8" green ball, cut it in half, and add eyes. Make an orange bill 1-1/2" long and 3/8" thick.
3. Position the pieces on the covered pen barrel. To form the mouth, cut the bill in half and add a red tongue. Decorate the bird further with red coils of clay or red dots. Use a round toothpick to make a series of holes in the back of the head and on the wings. After baking, the ends of the feathers can be inserted in the holes and secured with white craft glue.

How to Make the Base:

1. Trim the pen cap.
2. Wrap the cap with a sheet of orange clay. Smooth out the seam.
3. Make four orange teardrop-shaped clay pieces and four white teardrop-shaped clay pieces. The pieces need to be large enough to keep the stand steady while it holds the pen.
4. Position the pieces around the closed end of the cap to form a bird's foot and make the pen stand. ❑

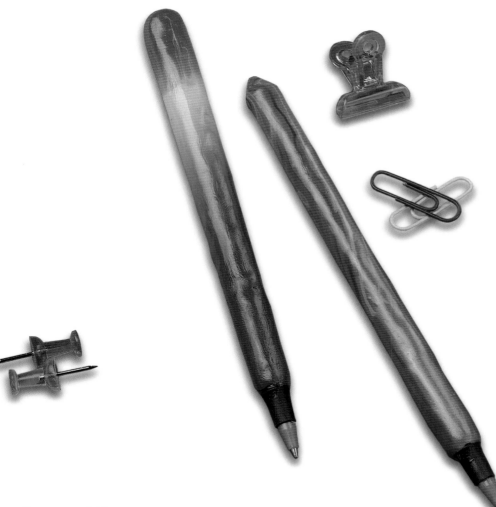

Covered Pens

You can blend colored clay to make a rainbow pen or use false wood clay or marble metallic clay to make elegant covered pens.

Feathered Bird Pen

After baking the pen and stand and reassembling the pen, test it. If the stand, is not holding the pen steady, sand a bit of clay from the bottom. Make sure the pen fits firmly in the stand.

More Covered Pens

You can also make a wonderful feathered bird pen or snake pen complete with a stand. Pictured are two examples, a snake and a bird. To make the Snake Pen, follow the instructions for making a covered pen and coil a long piece of clay around the covered pen cap to construct the stand. Other pen designs in this book include ladybugs, critters, and animal prints.

Varnishing Pens:

To varnish baked pens, thread a wooden skewer into the pen barrel and hold the skewer while you apply the varnish. Place the wooden skewer into an aluminum pan with sand to hold while drying.

Saying Stones

These "rocks that talk" are wonderful accessories for potted plants. Mixing ordinary kitchen spices into translucent clay creates the rock-like appearance. The clay is wrapped around a foil core – so you use less clay and the stones are less expensive than if they were solid clay. Step by step instructions appear on the following page.

Using an alphabet stamp set and a black inkpad, you can imprint your favorite saying or inspirational words into the formed rock.

Here Are Some Suggestions:

Follow your dream	Believe in magic
Whatever	Totally awesome
Have courage	Peace
Dream on	Joy
Put on a happy face	Hope
Hang on	Love

Instructions begin on page 88.

Here's How:

1. Roll out some translucent clay and add some seasoning salt – 1 teaspoon per 1/2 ounce of clay.
2. Mix some poppy seeds into some clay. Marble the poppy seed clay and the spiced translucent clay together for a realistic look.
3. Roll the marbled clay flat to make a sheet.
4. Form a base by crumpling a piece of aluminum foil.

Option: Use a heart-shaped piece of foil to make a heart-shaped rock.

5. Wrap the clay sheet around the foil base. Smooth out any bumps or seams. Stamp the stone with the word or words of your choice, using alphabet stamps and black stamp pad. *Option:* Stamp images on your stone for a different look.
6. Bake. Baked stones have a rock-like appearance and will have darkened slightly during baking. ❑

Ancient Pots

These ancient-looking pots use the slab method and coil method, and the results mimic the look of pots our ancestors might have made long ago. The pots are shaped on recycled glass jars and small glass candle cups. This makes it very easy for children to create perfectly shaped pots that can, after baking, hold water. Using jars also allows children to be very creative without worrying about whether the pots will collapse during baking and limits the size of the pots to the size of the jars you provide.

The soft bulk terra cotta clay is the easiest and most economical clay to use for pots, but any polymer clay can be used.

Three Coil Pots

The two pots, *opposite page left and right* use the coil method over small glass candle holders. Simply roll narrow coils of clay and press them over the glass to cover the surface. Notice how the coils are curled and formed. The pot on the left was washed with a dark acrylic wash and sanded; the one on the right has an acrylic wash of a lighter color.

The raffia-wrapped pot, *center,* is also made using the coil method. After the coils were put on the base (a glass vase), they were smoothed together, creating a surface that can be decorated with a rubber stamp. A black acrylic wash was brushed on after baking to bring out the imprinted details. This pot was given a gloss varnish coating.

Two Slab Pots

The tall imprinted pot and the smaller gold pot, *pictured at right,* were fashioned using the slab method. This project uses recycled glass jars – you can even cover the metal lids. (This was done on the jar at left.) Use homemade texture tools, design tools, or prehistoric-theme rubber stamps to add primitive-looking designs to the clay. *Option:* Use a light or dark wash of acrylic paint or waterbase stain to bring out the imprinted designs.

Small clay handles were added to the taller pot. After baking, a made-to-match pendant was tied on with raffia.

African-style Masks

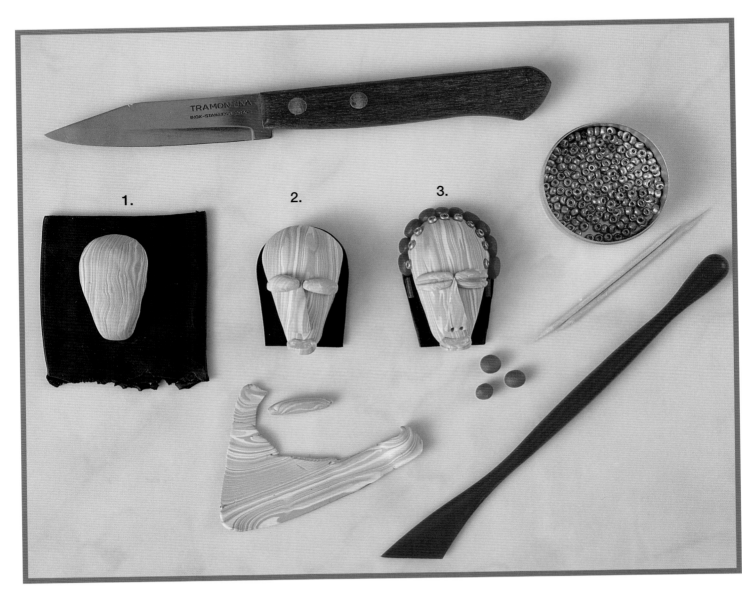

Here's How:

1. Make a base of crumpled foil and cover it with a sheet of "false wood" clay. (See the Basic Techniques section for instructions on making false wood clay.) Place the mask base on a piece of dark-colored clay sheet.

2. Trim this flat piece to create the back of the mask. Use the trimmings from the false wood clay to form the eyes, nose, and mouth. (This makes the mask look like it was carved.)

3. Add details to the features with a modeling tool or toothpick. Decorate the mask with glass beads and small pieces of clay. TIP: Use a wooden toothpick to pick up the small beads.

4. Bake. *Option:* Brush with a brown acrylic wash. Sand to bring out the details. ❏

These masks make great pendants for necklaces, lanyards for zipper pulls, or magnets. They are a suitable project for older children. Animal print beads are especially nice with masks. Use pictures of real African masks for inspiration while creating the masks. Masks can be made larger and used as decorative pieces to hang on a wall.

Patterns

Crayon Bookmark

Fountain Pen Bookmark

Patterns are actual size

Paint Brush Bookmark

Pencil Bookmark

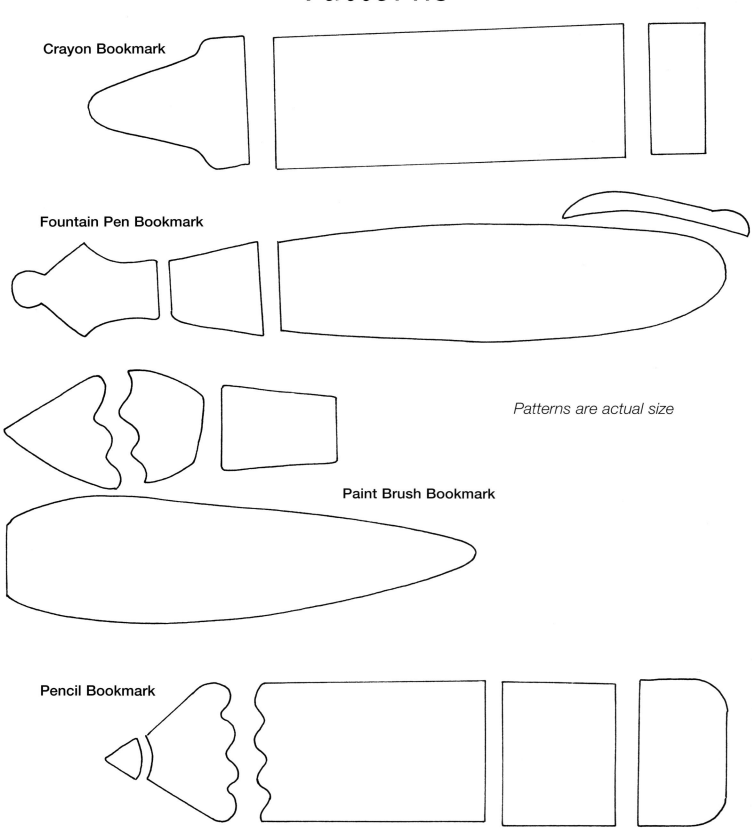

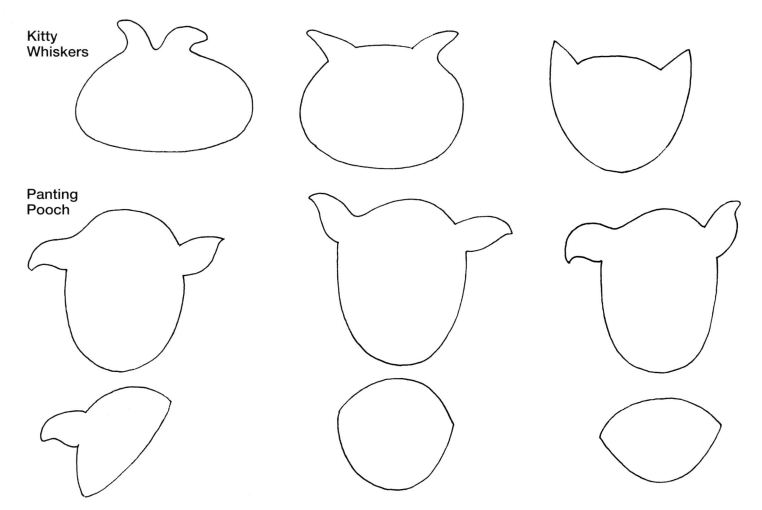

Kitty
Whiskers

Panting
Pooch

Metric Conversion Chart

Inches to Millimeters and Centimeters

Inches	MM	CM	Inches	MM	CM
1/8	3	.3	2	51	5.1
1/4	6	.6	3	76	7.6
3/8	10	1.0	4	102	10.2
1/2	13	1.3	5	127	12.7
5/8	16	1.6	6	152	15.2
3/4	19	1.9	7	178	17.8
7/8	22	2.2	8	203	20.3
1	25	2.5	9	229	22.9
1-1/4	32	3.2	10	254	25.4
1-1/2	38	3.8	11	279	27.9
1-3/4	44	4.4	12	305	30.5

Yards to Meters

Yards	Meters	Yards	Meters
1/8	.11	3	2.74
1/4	.23	4	3.66
3/8	.34	5	4.57
1/2	.46	6	5.49
5/8	.57	7	6.40
3/4	.69	8	7.32
7/8	.80	9	8.23
1	.91	10	9.14
2	1.83		

Index